The Changing Midwest Assessment:
Land Cover, Natural Resources, and People

Landscape Change

Executive Summary

Landscape change has emerged as one of the great issues of the day among scientists, land managers, elected officials and the public as it affects virtually all aspects of the biophysical and social landscape and impacts people from all walks of life. It is widely accepted that landscape change is the result of complex interactions between biological, physical, social, and economic factors, and that change is not random; however, a comprehensive study that documents the spatial distribution of change at the landscape scale has not been attempted, and the key drivers and consequences of change are not well understood.

In order to partially fill this gap we have developed a spatially explicit database that documents changes in land cover, forests, selected natural resources, and human demographics and attitudes across the seven States of the Midwest Region (figure 1). The resolution of measurement ranged from the county level to 1 km². In general, most attributes were monitored from roughly 1980 to 2000.

Land Cover

Land cover refers to the dominant feature on a given portion of the biophysical landscape. For example, a landscape that is dominated by trees would be classified as forestland.

The biophysical landscape of the Midwest was dominated by the agriculture and forestland cover types in 1980 and 2000. In absolute terms, the greatest changes in land cover were conversions from agriculture to forestland. The area of land classified as forestland increased by 2.86 million acres, equivalent to an average annual increase of 225 square miles of forestland between 1980 and 2000. On a percentage basis, the greatest change was from agriculture and forestland to urban. The urban land cover type increased 24.3 percent, equivalent to approximately 1.5 million acres.

Forests

The area, composition, and structure of midwestern forests changed rather dramatically between 1980 and 2000. The area of forest increased 7 percent, from 71.8 million acres in 1980 to 76.8 million acres in 2000. In terms of forest composition, which is a reference to the mix of tree species within a forest, Oak/Hickory remained the dominant forest type group, but Maple/Beech/Birch increased dramatically, and there were significant declines in Aspen/Birch and Spruce/Fir. Finally, the structure of forests, which has to do with the size of trees, underwent noticeable changes. In 1980, trees in the medium diameter stand-size class dominated the forests of the Midwest; in 2000, trees in the large diameter stand-size class were dominant.

Wildlife Indicator Species

In order to determine the impacts of landscape change on natural resources we monitored changes in animal species of special interest, including white-tailed deer and birds. In monitoring white-tailed deer, we tracked changes in total harvest, which increased nearly 250 percent between 1980 and 2000. In monitoring birds, we calculated changes in relative abundance. Across the Midwest, approximately 25 percent of bird species surveyed by the North American Breeding Bird Survey experienced significant declines.

Social Landscapes

Changes in human demographics between 1980 and 2000 included a 10-percent increase in population, a 22-percent increase in total housing density, and a 225-percent increase in the density of seasonal housing units. Attitudinal changes about urban sprawl indicate that concern about landscape change is on the rise. In fact, a series of surveys carried out by the Pew Center for Civic Journalism (2000) indicated that concern about sprawl was among the most frequently cited local problems in America.

Ongoing Research

In addition to documenting the spatial distribution of changes on the biophysical and social landscapes of the Midwest, this paper offers a brief description of ongoing research that is being conducted by scientists at the North Central Research Station and partner universities. These efforts include using remotely sensed land cover data to calculate historical and current levels of forest fragmentation; developing predictive models that simulate what future landscape will look like under various management strategies; determining the nature of the relationship between landscape change and changes in bird populations; developing fine-scale housing density projections decades into the future.

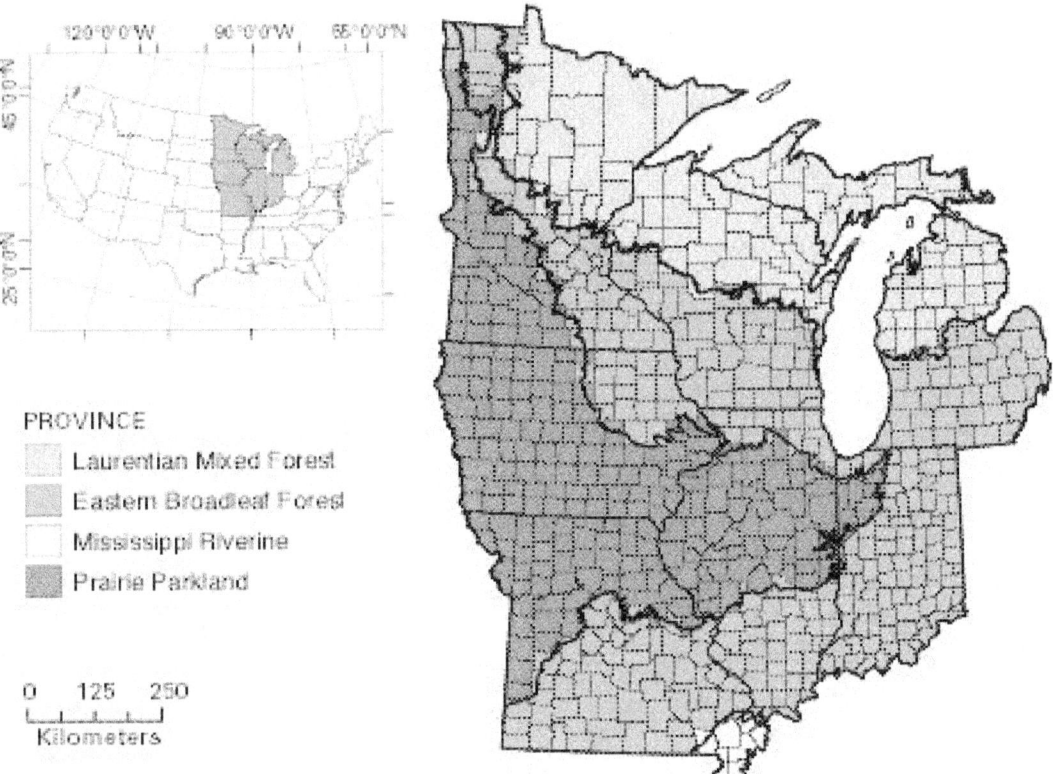

Figure 1 The seven States of the Midwest Region, by ecological province and county.

PROVINCE

- Laurentian Mixed Forest
- Eastern Broadleaf Forest
- Mississippi Riverine
- Prairie Parkland

0   125   250
Kilometers

Finally, we invite you to visit the Changing Midwest Web site (figure 2). The Web site expands on the material in this paper, provides the opportunity to view enlarged maps and graphics, and is continually updated: http://www.ncrs.fs.fed.us/4153/deltawest

Figure 2. Home page of the North Central Research Station Changing Midwest Web site.

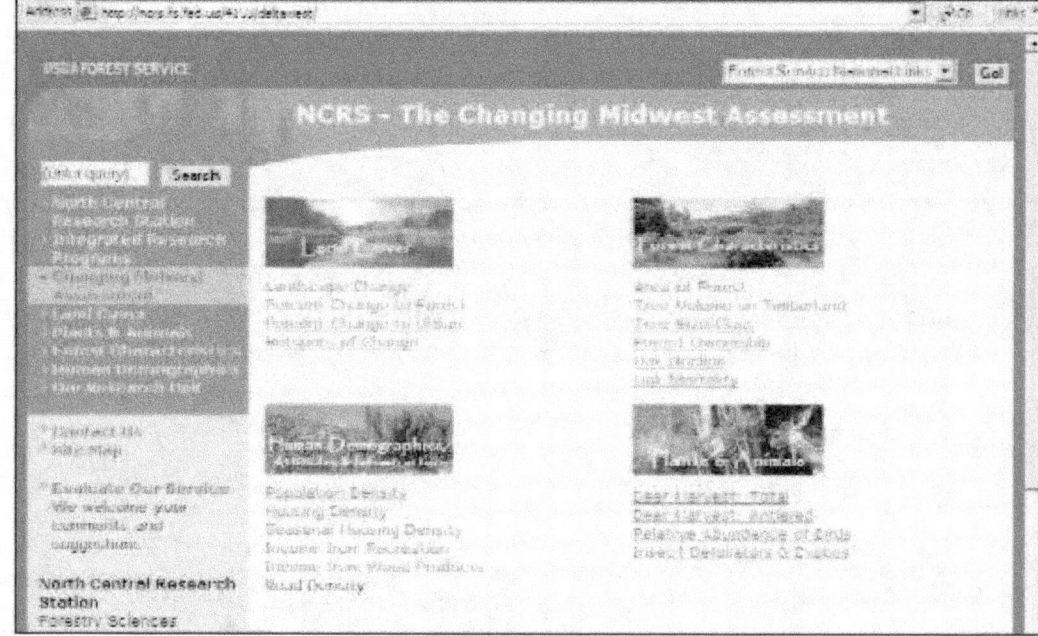

Introduction

In 2000, the North Central Research Station established the Landscape Change Integrated Research Program. The purpose of the program, which was born out of a comprehensive review of the major issues facing our clients and the resources of the region, was to encourage the establishment of inter-disciplinary teams of scientists who would study landscape change collaboratively and, in so doing, develop a holistic understanding of the issues surrounding landscape change and knowledge and tools that resource managers, elected officials, and the public can use to make informed choices about how we use natural resources. Based on a series of workshops that included Station scientists and interested stakeholders, the following overarching objectives were identified:

1. To characterize the current patterns of land use and land cover change across the seven States of the Midwest Region (figure 1);

2. To understand the physical, biological, social, and economic factors influencing the rate and extent of landscape change;

3. To determine the effects of landscape change on people and ecosystems; and

4. To assess the effectiveness of public policies that aim to regulate landscape change.

This paper summarizes the Assessment phase (Objective 1) of the program by featuring selected variables that describe changes in land cover, forest characteristics, natural resources, human demographics, and attitudes about landscape change. To view a complete project report, visit the Changing Midwest Web site at: www.ncrs.fs.fed.us/4153/deltawest (figure 2).

Land Cover

Land cover data provide a "big picture" snapshot of the landscape, classifying tracts of land based on the distribution of dominant cover types. The major land cover types in the region are agriculture, forest, wetland, water, urban, and barren. We focused on changes in agriculture, forest, and urban cover types. Data collection and analysis were accomplished in association with the University of Michigan School of Natural Resources and the Environment (www.snre.umich.edu/).

Forests

We assessed several forest characteristics, including area, composition, structure, and ownership. Change is reported for all forested land and by forest type group. Data were retrieved from the USDA Forest Service North Central Research Station Forest Inventory and Analysis Database (www.ncrs.fs.fed.us/4801/tools-data/data).

Wildlife Indicator Species

We assessed changes in white-tailed deer and selected resident and migrant songbirds that breed in the region. Data were retrieved and analyzed in association with state natural resource management agencies, and John Sauer at the USGS Patuxent Wildlife Research Center (www.pwrs.usgs.gov).

Social Landscapes

The human demographic characteristics we monitored include population density, total and seasonal housing density, and personal income from forestry, lumber and wood products, and recreation. We used data from the U.S. Census Bureau and the U.S. Bureau of Economic Analysis. Data retrieval and analysis was accomplished in association with the Applied Population Laboratory at the University of Wisconsin-Madison (www.ssc.wisc.edu/poplab/).

We also identified specific concerns that people have about urban sprawl and monitored how those concerns varied spatially and temporally. Data retrieval and analysis were accomplished in association with collaborators at the University of Minnesota, using the Lexis-Nexis online database, and InfoTrend software.

Ongoing Research

Finally, this paper offers a glimpse into ongoing research at the North Central Research Station. Brief descriptions of these studies, as well as a glossary of terms and other reference materials, are located at the end of this document.

How to Contact Us

It is not our intent to characterize change as "good" or "bad." Rather, our aim has been to provide the public, resource professionals, and elected officials with data on how the landscape is changing so they can make informed decisions. We hope you find this assessment useful, and that you will contact any of the authors if you have questions or suggestions.

To obtain contact information for the authors of this paper, visit our Web site at www.ncrs.fs.fed.us and select **Contact Us.** To learn more about these and other studies, visit the Web sites of our individual research work units, which can be accessed at the same site by navigating to **Research Work Units.**

Introduction

Since the 1930s the Forest Inventory and Analysis (FIA) research unit of the Forest Service has monitored *land use* across the seven States comprising the Midwest Region. For the most part, FIA has focused on the extent and condition of public and private forests. In recent years, however, the factors that influence forests have become so complex that it is necessary to look beyond land use within the forest boundary to effectively manage forests. In particular, we need to integrate the consideration of *land cover* data, including non-forestland cover types, into our decision-making processes.

The primary differences between land use and land cover data are scale related. Land use data are very specific, whereas land cover data provide a big picture view of the landscape. For example, forestland use data will contain detailed stand and tree level information about the extent, composition, and structure of forests. Land cover data describe a landscape in terms of physical features that dominate it. Forestland, then, is land that is dominated by trees. The six major land cover types in the region are agriculture, forestland, wetland, urban, water, and barren.

This analysis focuses on three cover types: agriculture, forestland, and urban. The agriculture cover type is land used primarily for food and fiber production and is composed of cropland, pasture, orchards, groves, vineyards, and other non-tree-based agricultural crops. The forestland cover type is land dominated by trees. As a general rule, a tract of land must be at least 40 percent covered by tree canopies to be classified as forestland. The urban cover type is characterized by buildings, roads, and vegetation indicative of human settlement and industrial or commercial activity.

In analyzing land cover, we sought to answer three main questions:

- How has land cover changed?

- How has forestland cover changed?

- How has urban land cover changed?

Detecting Land Cover Change

We developed a novel image processing approach to detect land cover change across the seven States of the Midwest Region between 1980 and 2000. To do so, we used a USGS National Aerial Photography Program (NAPP) photo-derived national land cover classification from 1980 (Land Use and Land Cover or LUDA), combined with National Oceanic and

Landscape change is not random. It is possible to identify the "drivers" of change, predict where future change is likely to occur, and craft **strategic responses.**

Atmospheric Administration (NOAA) Advanced Very High Resolution Radiometer (AVHRR) Normalized Difference Vegetation Index (NDVI) time series satellite imagery from 2000 to identify areas where substantial changes occurred within and among agriculture, forestland, and urban cover types. In order to achieve accurate data comparability we implemented three new approaches to merging heterogeneous spatial data sets for change analysis. First, we developed a 2000 satellite image ISODATA classification in a way that approximated the 1980 photo-interpreted classifications as closely as possible. Next, we used a third, independent data set that was collected consistently across the time period to constrain and improve comparability. Finally, we combined these products in an allocation procedure (Bergen *et al.* 2002).

Land Cover Maps

We produced land cover maps for 1980 and 2000 (figure 3) and a series of change maps (figures 4, 11, and 17). The 1980 and 2000 land cover maps show the spatial distribution of land cover types that were dominant at a resolution of 1 km^2. Thus, for example, a tract of land classified as forestland was not necessarily 100 percent forested; rather, trees were the dominant feature over that 1-km^2 area.

The first change map (figure 4) shows where dominant land cover changed from one type to another at a resolution of 1 km^2. Figures 11 and 17 show conversion to forestland and urban types, respectively, at a resolution of 25 km^2. Collectively, these figures provide an excellent snapshot of the spatial distribution of the major land cover types across the region, and estimates of the area of land in each cover type and the rate and spatial distribution of conversions between cover types.

The Nature of Land Cover Change

Although identifying and mapping changes in land cover is no small feat, it is actually just the first step in the process of understanding why landscape change occurs, what the ecological, economic, and social consequences are, where it is likely to occur in the future, and how landscapes can be managed now in order to preserve that which we value for future generations. In the pages that follow, we will present maps that depict where change occurred and offer our interpretation of what it means. Although it is not our intention to characterize change as "good" or "bad," it is clear that the public is concerned about landscape change. In fact, a recent series of surveys carried out by the Pew Center for Civic Journalism (2000) indicated that concerns about "growth" and "sprawl-related" issues were tied with "crime and violence" as the most frequently mentioned local problems. For that reason, we offer the following "take home" message upfront as encouragement: Landscape change is not random. It is possible to identify the "drivers" of change, predict where future change is likely to occur, and craft strategic responses.

Dominant Land Cover: 1980 and 2000

In 1980, the most prevalent land cover type in the region was agriculture (figure 3, 1980). Over 65 percent of the land base was dedicated to the production of cultivated crops (including "row" and "close grown" crops like corn, soybeans, and wheat) and noncultivated crops (including permanent hayland and perennial horticultural crops such as strawberries). The next most prevalent land cover type was forestland. Approximately 29 percent of the region was classified as forestland. In order, other land cover types that were dominant at a resolution of 1 km were urban, water, wetland, and barren. Collectively, they were the dominant cover types on less than 6 percent of the landscape.

Similarly, the most prevalent land cover types in the region in 2000 were agriculture and forestland (figure 3, 2000). Together, they dominated approximately 94 percent of the land base in the region. In order, other land cover types that were dominant at a resolution of 1 km were urban, water, wetland, and barren. Collectively, they were the dominant cover type on approximately 6 percent of the landscape.

1980   **2000**

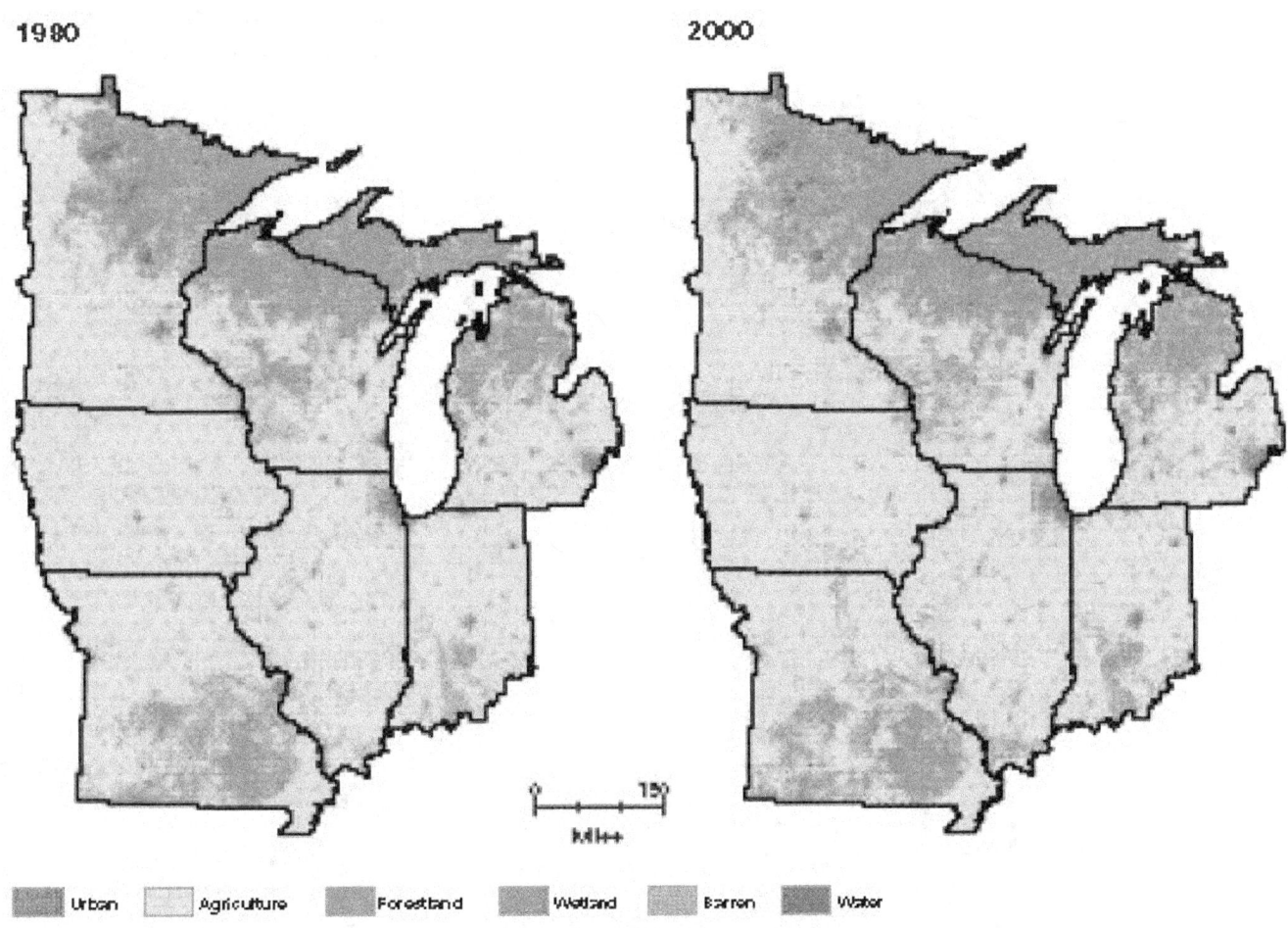

Urban   Agriculture   Forestland   Wetland   Barren   Water

Figure 3. Distribution of dominant land cover types in the Midwest Region (1 km), 1980 and 2000.

How Has Land Cover Changed?

How has land cover in the Midwest Region changed? Overall, the area of land in each of the major land cover types remained relatively stable between 1980 and 2000. In fact, the 1980 and 2000 land cover maps (figure 3) appear identical at first glance.

To fully understand how land cover changed, however, we need to consider not just area, but also spatial distribution. Figure 4 shows where change occurred. Region wide, percent change to urban (24.3-percent increase), to forestland (3.7-percent increase), and from agriculture (2.4-percent decrease) were the most common changes in land cover between 1980 and 2000.

Change

No Change   To Forestland   To Barren
To Agriculture   To Wetland   To Urban

Figure 4. Spatial distribution of changes in dominant land cover at a resolution of 1 km, 1980-2000. For example, each red pixel identifies a 1-km² parcel of land that was converted 'to urban' at some point between 1980 and 2000.

At the State level (figure 5), the increase in urban cover type ranged from 10.8 percent in Iowa (roughly 44,478 acres) to 32.0 percent in Michigan (414,881 acres). Change in agriculture cover type ranged from an 8.0-percent decrease in Michigan (roughly 1.25 million acres) to a 0.6-percent decrease in Iowa (roughly 200,645 acres). Change in forestland cover type ranged from a 1.0-percent increase in Indiana (roughly 33,359 acres) to an 11.5-percent increase in Iowa (roughly 170,499 acres).

Region wide, agricultural land decreased by 4.2 million acres, with most reverting to forestland or being converted to urban cover. Forestland increased by 2.86 million acres and urban cover increased by 1.45 million acres.

Overall, the area of land in each of the major land cover types remained relatively stable between 1980 and 2000. To fully understand how land cover changed, however, we need to consider not just area, but also spatial distribution.

Interpreting Land Cover Change

To put this into perspective, consider that the area of agricultural land decreased by 4.2 million acres, most of which reverted to forestland or was converted to urban. The area of forestland increased by 2.86 million acres and the area of land classified as urban increased by 1.45 million acres.

Region wide, three trends in land cover change emerged. The corn and soybean belts in Illinois and Iowa and the forestland in northern Minnesota, Wisconsin, and Michigan remained relatively stable (figure 6, Shenandoah, IA).

On the other hand, productive agricultural land associated with industrial/high-tech areas experienced moderate levels of change, primarily being converted to the urban cover type. Marginally productive agricultural land also experienced moderate levels of change, frequently reverting to forestland (figure 6, Dixon Springs, IL).

Finally, urban and suburban areas associated with large cities experienced significant levels of large-scale change, particularly along water and rail transportation routes (figure 6, Ann Arbor, MI). To view additional change maps, please visit the Changing Midwest Web site at www.ncrs.fs.fed.us/4153/deltawest and select Hotspots of Change.

Overall, land cover remained relatively stable. The region was dominated by agriculture and forestland in 1980 and it was dominated by agriculture and forestland to an even greater extent in 2000. Of course, such a "big picture" view only provides part of the answer.

Percent Change

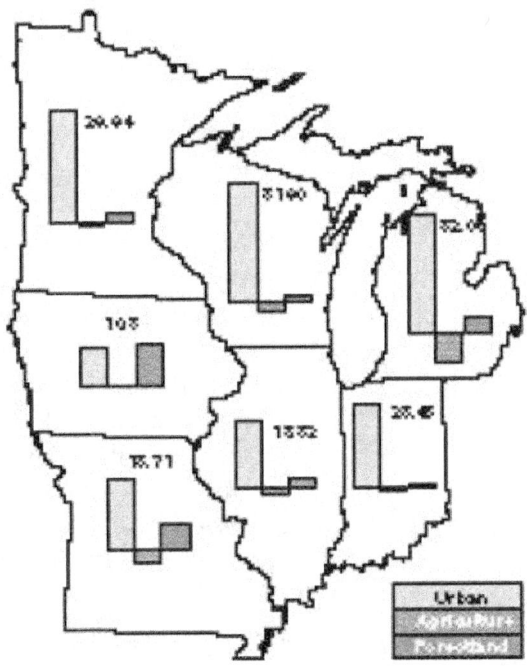

Figure 5. Percent change in urban, agriculture, and forestland cover types, 1980-2000. Value corresponds with the cover type that experienced the greatest amount of change.

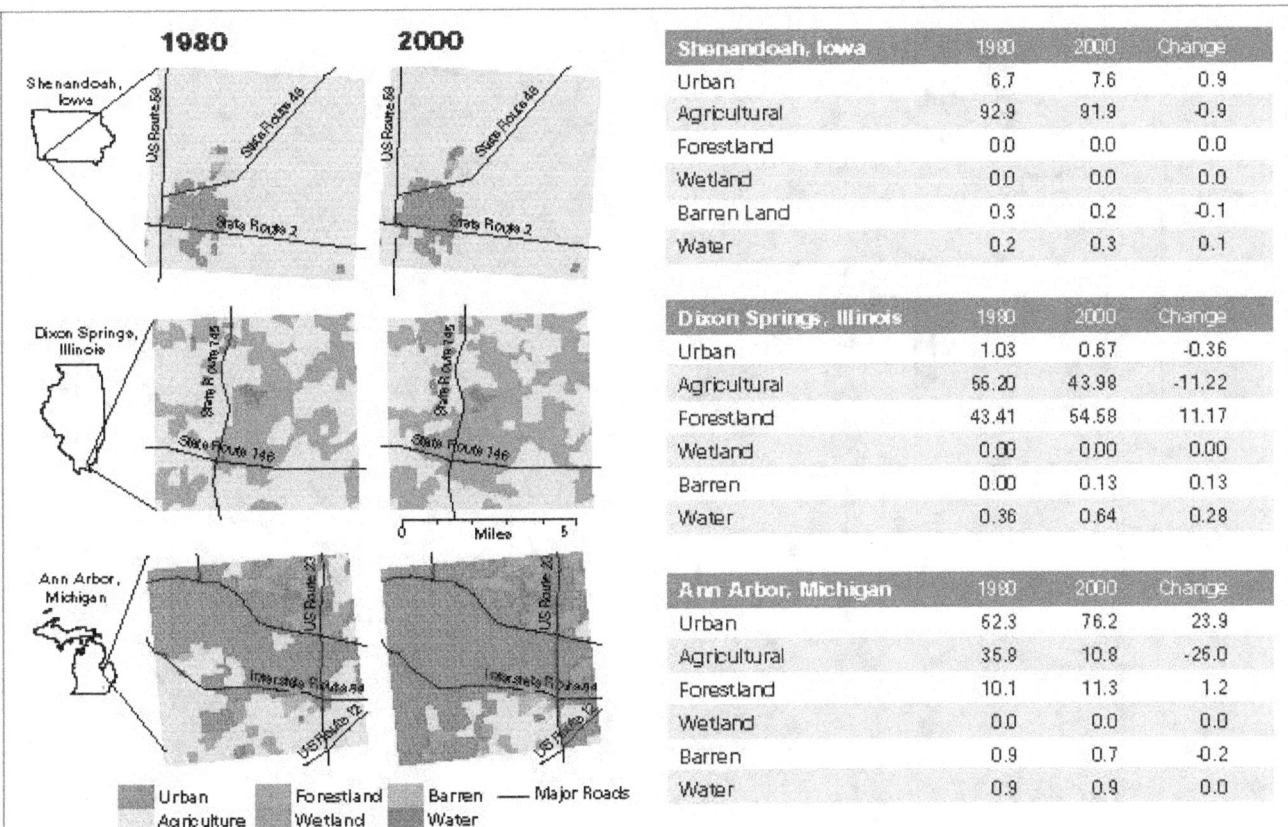

Shenandoah, Iowa	1980	2000	Change
Urban	6.7	7.6	0.9
Agricultural	92.9	91.9	-0.9
Forestland	0.0	0.0	0.0
Wetland	0.0	0.0	0.0
Barren Land	0.3	0.2	-0.1
Water	0.2	0.3	0.1

Dixon Springs, Illinois	1980	2000	Change
Urban	1.03	0.67	-0.36
Agricultural	55.20	43.98	-11.22
Forestland	43.41	54.58	11.17
Wetland	0.00	0.00	0.00
Barren	0.00	0.13	0.13
Water	0.36	0.64	0.28

Ann Arbor, Michigan	1980	2000	Change
Urban	52.3	76.2	23.9
Agricultural	35.8	10.8	-25.0
Forestland	10.1	11.3	1.2
Wetland	0.0	0.0	0.0
Barren	0.9	0.7	-0.2
Water	0.9	0.9	0.0

Figure 6. Region-wide trends in land cover conversions. Examples of high (Ann Arbor), medium (Dixon Springs), and low (Shenandoah) change landscapes. Table indicates percent of land that was dominated by each cover type, and percent change between 1980 and 2000.

How Has Forestland Cover Changed?

Anyone who has attended a Forest Service public hearing related to logging can attest to the fact that the folks who participate in those meetings are very concerned about public forestland. The meetings are often extremely tense and punctuated by inflammatory rhetorical exchanges between "environmentalists" and "resource developers." It would be reasonable to assume that the sides are arguing about how much forestland is remaining, but, if that were the case, the debate would be very short. So, how has the area of forestland in the Midwest changed? Once again, the answer will likely surprise many.

Area of Forestland: 1980

In 1980, forestland was identified as the dominant cover type across more than 76.8 million acres (28.8 percent of the region). Forestland was most abundant in the northern tier of the Lakes States, and to a lesser degree in southern Missouri and Indiana (figure 3).

At the State level, the percentage of land classified as forestland ranged from 4.1 percent in Iowa to 51.5 percent in Michigan (figure 7). The area of forestland ranged from 1.5 million acres in Iowa to 19.1 million acres in Michigan (figure 8).

Area of Forestland: 2000

In 2000, forestland was identified as the dominant cover type across more than 79.6 million acres (29.9 percent of the region). Once again, forestland was most abundant in the northern tier of the Lakes States and in Missouri and southern Indiana (figure 3).

Percent Forestland

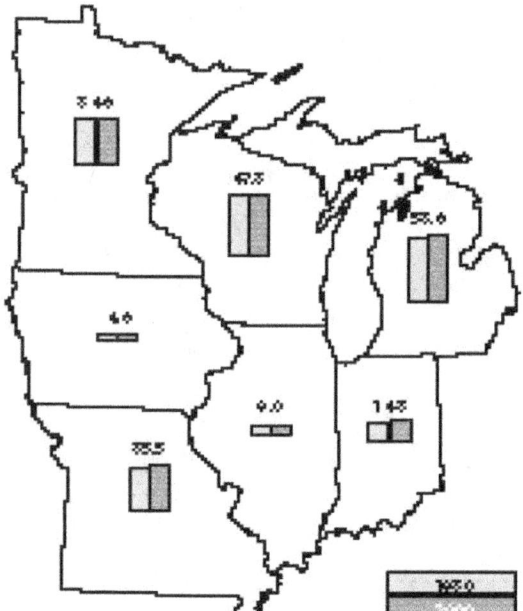

Figure 7. Percent of land classified as forestland, 1980 and 2000. Value corresponds with the year in which forestland comprised the greater proportion of the total land area.

Area of Forestland
(million acres)

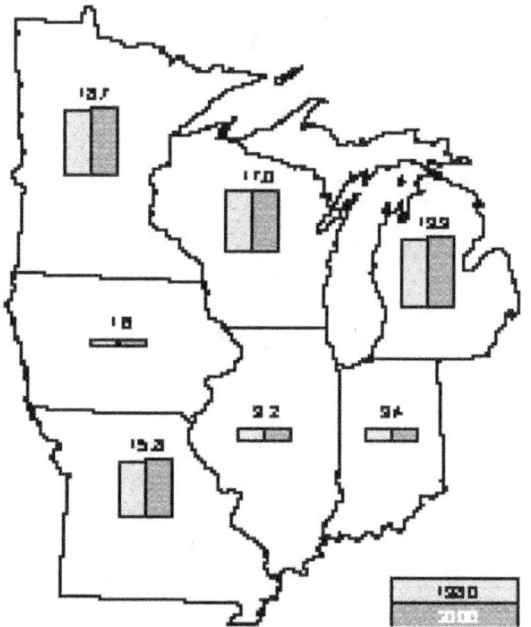

Figure 8. Area of land classified as forestland (million acres), 1980 and 2000. Value corresponds with the year that had the greater amount of forestland.

At the State level, the percentage of land classified as forestland ranged from 4.6 percent in
Iowa to 53.6 percent in Michigan (figure 7).
The area of forestland ranged from 1.6 million
acres in Iowa to 19.9 million acres in Michigan
(figure 8).

Percent Change in Forestland

Region wide, the area of forestland increased by
3.7 percent. In absolute terms, the area of forestland increased by 2.86 million acres between
1980 and 2000, which, on average, is equivalent to an annual increase of nearly 225 square
miles of forestland.

At the State level, percent change in the area of
forestland ranged from a 1.0-percent increase in
Indiana to an increase of 11.5 percent in Iowa

(figure 9). To put this into perspective, consider
that annual change in the area of forestland
ranged from an increase of 1,668 acres in
Indiana to an increase of 53,262 acres in
Missouri (figure 10).

Rate of Conversion to Forestland

Region wide, the rate of conversion from non-
forest to forestland ranged from less than 10
percent to more than 50 percent at a resolution
of 25 km² (figure 11). To put this into perspective, consider that each pixel or cell in figure 11
represents approximately 6,178 acres, and that
each dark green cell represents the conversion of
no less than 3,000 acres from a non-forestland
cover type to the forestland cover type at some
point between 1980 and 2000.

Percent Change

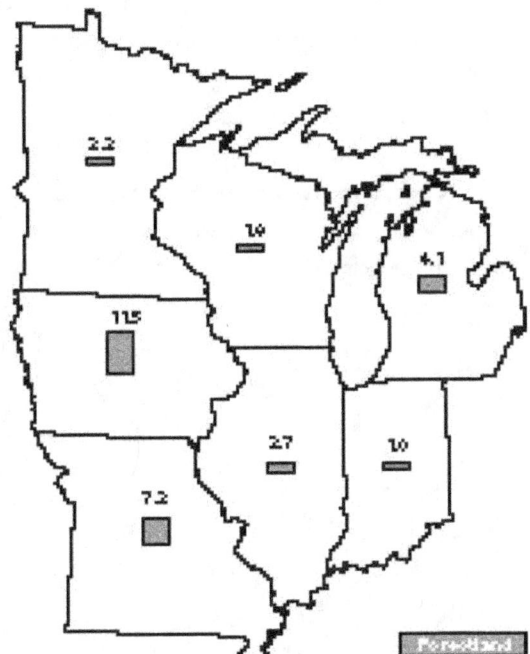

Figure 9. Percent change in the area of land classified as forestland,
1980-2000.

Change
(acres/year)

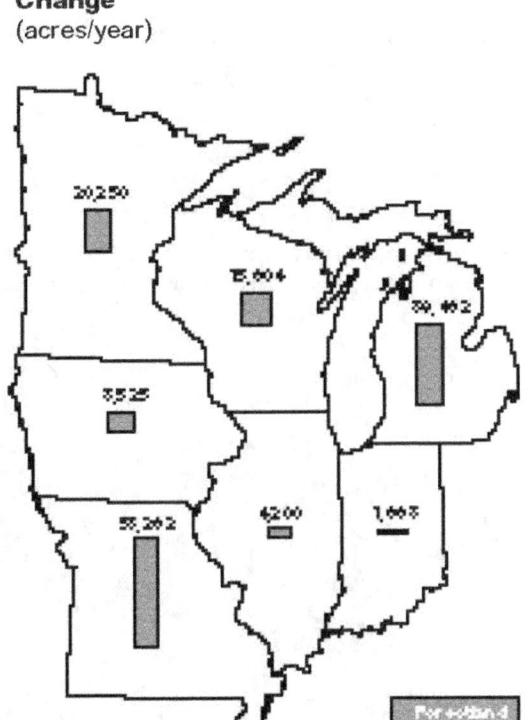

Figure 10. Annual change in area of land classified as forestland, 1980-2000.

Percent Change

	No Change		10 - 20		30 - 40
	<10%		20 - 30		40 - 50
					> 50%

Figure 11. Percent change to forestland, 1980-2000. Map colors correspond to the proportion of each 25-km² cell that was converted to forestland.

How has the area of forestland in the Midwest changed? Once again, the answer will likely surprise many people. Region-wide, the area of forestland as a dominant land cover type increased by 3.7 percent, which is equivalent to 2.86 million acres. The rate of conversion from non-forest to forestland ranged from less than 10 percent to more than 50 percent at a resolution of 25 km².

Interpreting Change in Forestland Cover

In order to interpret these data correctly it is important to remember that they describe the spatial distribution of forestland as a dominant land cover type, as opposed to the spatial distribution of forest, which is a type of land use. The forestland cover data presented here and the forest land use data presented in a later chapter are, in fact, highly correlated (see figures 7 and 19 and figures 8 and 20), but one should not expect them to be equivalent or be alarmed by differences. Land cover data provide a big picture view of the landscape, whereas land use data provide, in the case of forest, highly detailed information at scales as fine as the individual tree. Bearing this in mind, consider the following images, which depict a landscape that experienced significant changes in forestland (figure 12). In particular, note the conversion from agriculture (depicted in yellow) to forest (depicted in green) and urban (depicted in red).

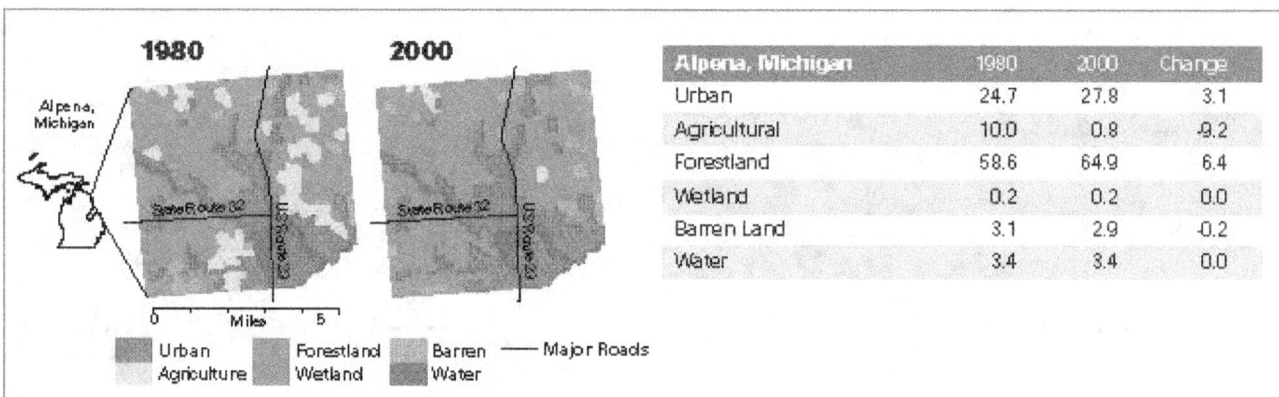

Alpena, Michigan	1980	2000	Change
Urban	24.7	27.8	3.1
Agricultural	10.0	0.8	-9.2
Forestland	58.6	64.9	6.4
Wetland	0.2	0.2	0.0
Barren Land	3.1	2.9	-0.2
Water	3.4	3.4	0.0

Figure 12. Spatial distribution and intensity of change in dominant landcover in Alpena, Michigan, 1980-2000. Table indicates proportion of landscape that was dominated by each cover type, and percent change between 1980 and 2000.

How Has Urban Land Cover Changed?

Whether you think of it as "development" or "urban sprawl" one thing is certain–it is happening all across the Midwest. Or is it? The following images (figures 15-17) clearly depict a landscape that is becoming more developed. However, the base land cover maps (figure 3) just as clearly depict that the landscape of the Midwest was dominated by agriculture and forest in both 1980 and 2000, and the landscape change map (figure 4) suggests that the proportion of the landscape that was dominated by agriculture and forest actually increased between 1980 and 2000. So, the question stands: Is the landscape of the Midwest becoming more rural or more urban? In truth, the answer largely depends on how urban and forestland are defined.

As noted, urban land is land that is characterized by a mixture of buildings, conveyances, and associated vegetation that are indicative of human settlement and/or industrial or commercial activity. Forestland is land that has an aerial crown density or canopy closure of at least 40 percent. Based on these definitions, forestland experienced the greatest increase in area among dominant land cover types. In fact, the area of forestland increased by nearly twice as much as the area of land classified as urban. So, on one hand, an argument could be made that the landscape of the Midwest actually became more rural between 1980 and 2000. On the other hand, while some of the lands that converted to forestland had been classified as urban, most of the land had been in agriculture, including cropland, pastureland, and rangeland. In other words, there was only a modest net increase in the area of rural land. Conversely, most of the land that converted to urban had been classified as forest or agriculture. Hence, a conservative

interpretation of these data suggests that the land cover of the Midwest remained relatively stable over the past two decades, becoming only slightly more rural.

While this interpretation of landscape change is technically correct, we recognize that it will not be emotionally satisfying or consistent with the perceptions of many people. There are many people who feel that "sprawl" is overtaking the landscape. In part, these inconsistencies are likely due to differences in the technical definition of urban and forestland and the layperson's definition of these terms. For example, consider that even if a parcel of land is completely forested, meaning that it has a canopy closure of at least 90 percent, it is entirely possible that a significant "swing set understory" of permanent and/or seasonal homes is present. Given a canopy closure of 90 percent the land would be classified as forestland. However, given the presence of a significant "swing set understory," the layperson might reasonably ask, "Is this forest really a forest or is it urban?" The point of this discussion is not to discredit our data or interpretation. We have full confidence in our data. In fact, data collected by field survey crews paint a similar picture. However, in the spirit of contributing to a fully informed discussion about landscape change, it is right and proper to disclose that remotely sensed land cover data might underestimate the actual extent of urban development given that understory development cannot be readily detected remotely. Further, it highlights the value of studying landscape change through an interdisciplinary lens, and we encourage people to consider additional sources of information when thinking about these issues, including the forest characteristics data presented in the following section of this paper.

Urban Land Cover: 1980

Region wide, urban was identified as the dominant land cover type on approximately 6 million acres (2.2 percent of the region). At the
State level, the percentage of land classified as
urban ranged from less than 1 percent in
Minnesota to 4 percent in Illinois (figure 13).
The area of land classified as urban ranged
from 412,000 acres in Iowa to 1.4 million acres
in Illinois (figure 14).

Urban Land Cover: 2000

Urban was identified as the dominant land
cover type on 7.4 million acres (approximately
2.8 percent of the region). At the State level,
the percentage of land classified as urban
ranged from 1.3 percent in Iowa and
Minnesota to 4.8 percent in Illinois and
Indiana (figure 13). The area of land classified
as urban ranged from 456,000 acres in Iowa to
1.7 million acres in Illinois (figure 14).

Percent Urban

Figure 13. Percent of total land area classified as urban, 1980 and 2000. Value
corresponds with the year in which urban comprised the greater proportion of the
total land area.

Area of Urban
(million acres)

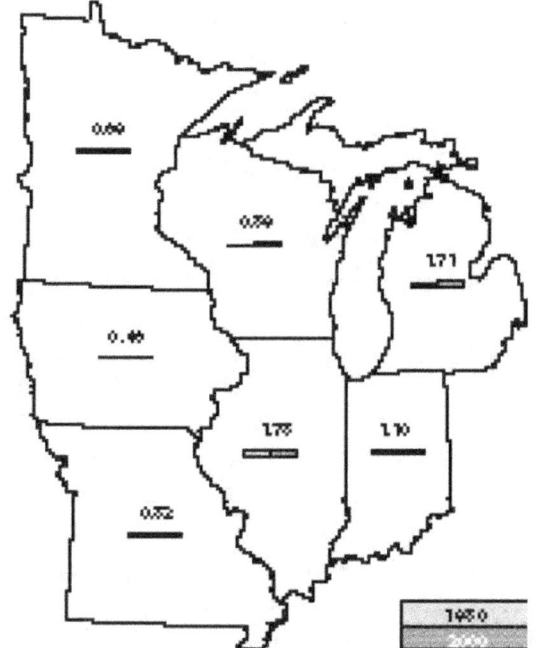

Figure 14. Area of land classified as urban (million acres), 1980
and 2000.

Percent Change to Urban

Region wide, the area of land classified as urban increased by roughly 1.5 million acres (24.3 percent) between 1980 and 2000. The area of urban land cover increased in each of the seven Midwestern States, ranging from an increase of 10.8 percent in Iowa to an increase of 32.0 percent in Michigan (figure 15). In absolute terms, the greatest change occurred in Michigan where the area of urban land cover increased by nearly 415,000 acres. To put this into perspective, consider that average annual change in the area of urban land cover ranged from 2,224 acres in Iowa to nearly 21,000 acres in Michigan (figure 16).

Rate of Conversion to Urban

One of the most troubling aspects about landscape change is the rate of "urban sprawl." In municipalities experiencing sprawl, the rate of conversion from non-urban land cover types, primarily agriculture and forestland, to urban ranged from less than 5 percent to more than 20 percent. To put this into perspective, consider that each dark red cell on the Change map (figure 17) represents the conversion of at least 1,500 acres from a non-urban cover type to the urban cover type (i.e., 25 percent of a 25-km^2 cell).

Percent Change

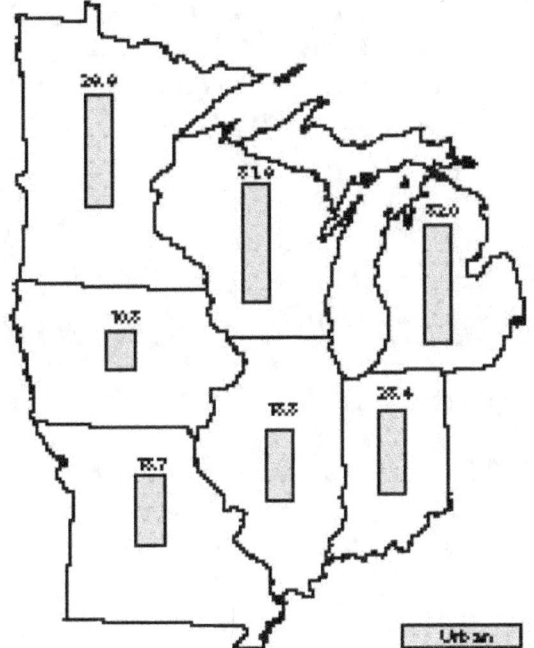

Figure 15. Percent change in the area of land classified as urban, 1980-2000.

**Change
(acres/year)**

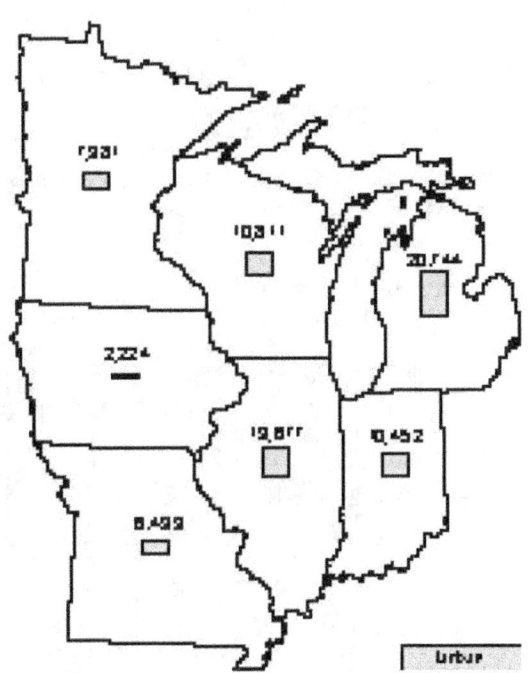

Figure 16. Annual change in the area of land classified as urban, 1980-2000.

Percent Change

No Change	5 - 10	15 - 20
<5%	10 - 15	20 - 25
		>25%

Figure 17. Percent change to urban, 1980-2000. Map colors correspond to the proportion of each 25-km² cell that was converted "to urban."

Is the landscape of the Midwest becoming more rural or more urban? In lieu of providing the "right" answer, we offer the following technical interpretation of how the land cover of the Midwest changed between 1980 and 2000. In absolute terms, forestland experienced the greatest increase in area. Among dominant land cover types, urban had the highest rate of conversion. Finally, it warrants repeating that our measurement of land cover likely underestimated the actual extent of urban development given that understory development cannot be detected remotely.

Understanding Urban Sprawl

In some respects, explaining urban sprawl is simple. For example, it is clear that most of the significant conversions to urban occurred on the fringe of large metropolitan areas that are serviced by major water and transportation routes (figure 18). On the other hand, we have much to learn about the causes and consequence of sprawl. To learn more about ongoing research related to urban sprawl, visit our Web site at www.ncrs.fs.fed.us/4153/deltawest.

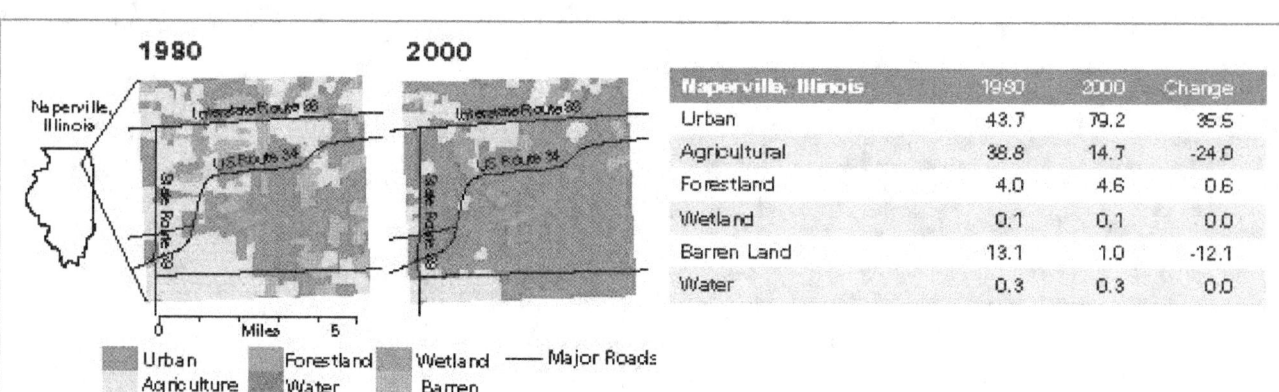

Naperville, Illinois	1980	2000	Change
Urban	43.7	79.2	35.5
Agricultural	38.8	14.7	-24.0
Forestland	4.0	4.6	0.6
Wetland	0.1	0.1	0.0
Barren Land	13.1	1.0	-12.1
Water	0.3	0.3	0.0

Figure 18. Spatial distribution and intensity of change in dominant land cover in Naperville, Illinois, 1980-2000. Table indicates percent of landscape that was dominated by each cover type, and percent change between 1980 and 2000.

Introduction

In Section 1 we described the spatial distribution of dominant land cover types, including forestland. Here we describe the spatial distribution of forest as a type of land use. These data are highly correlated (see figures 7 and 19 and figures 8 and 20), but they are not equivalent. As noted, land cover data provide a big picture view of the landscape, whereas forest land use data provide detailed information at scales as fine as the individual tree.

The Forest Inventory and Analysis research unit defines forest as a tract of land that is at least 10 percent stocked with live forest trees of any size, or formerly having had such tree cover, and not currently developed for nonforest use. Stocking is determined by comparing site-specific standards for basal area and/or number of trees, age or size, and spacing against what is actually on the ground. For additional information about site-specific standards, contact the FIA research unit at www.ncrs.fs.fed.us/4801. The minimum area for classification as forest is 1 acre. Roadside, streamside, and shelterbelt strips that are wooded must have a crown width of at least 120 feet for a continuous length of 363 feet to qualify as forest. Unimproved roads and trails, streams, or other bodies of water or clearings in forest areas are classified as forest if less than 120 feet wide or smaller than 1 acre (Miles *et al.* 2001).

We evaluated changes in the forests of the region between roughly 1980 and 2000 (Appendix A) using the Forest Inventory and Analysis database (FIADB), which can be accessed online at www.ncrs.fs.fed.us/4801. Although there are many ways to characterize the changes that the forests of the Midwest have undergone over the past 20 years, we organized this summary according to common questions that people ask about forests:

- How has the area of forest changed?

- How has the composition of forests changed?

- How has the structure of forests changed?

- Who owns the forests of the Midwest?

How Much Forest is There?

The measure of "how much" that people are typically interested in is the area of forest. Forest is defined as land that is minimally stocked with trees of any size, or land that formerly had such tree cover, which has not been converted to a nonforest use. We calculated change in the total area of forest and the area of forest by forest type group.

How Has the Composition of Forests Changed?

Forest composition is a reference to the mix of tree species within a forest. In the Midwest there are 125 species of trees, each of which has been assigned to one or more of 28 forest type groups. Forest type groups are comprised of trees that share similar characteristics and habitat requirements. For example, the Oak/Hickory forest type group is comprised of various species of oak and hickory trees that are commonly found growing together. Following this example, a forest would be classified as Oak/Hickory if the plurality of trees were associated with the Oak/Hickory forest type group. We calculated change in the most common forest type groups in the region including, Oak/Hickory, Maple/Beech/Birch, Aspen/Birch, Spruce/Fir, and Elm/Ash/Cottonwood.

How Has the Structure of Forests Changed?

The structure of a forest has to do with the age, size, and spatial arrangement of the trees within. Of these structural characteristics, size is the most readily recognizable. The USDA Forest Service recognizes three stand-size classes: large, medium, and small. Stand-size is determined by the ratio of large-, medium-, and small-diameter trees on a given tract of land. Suffice it to say that large-diameter trees are most prevalent in large-diameter stands, and so forth. We calculated change in the prevalence of all large-, medium-, and small-diameter stands on all timberland, and change in the prevalence of large-, medium-, and small-diameter stands on all timberland by forest type group. Timberland is forest land that is producing, or is capable of producing, in excess of 20 cubic feet per acre per year of industrial roundwood products under natural conditions, is not withdrawn from timber utilization by statute or administrative regulation, and is not associated with urban or rural development.

Who Owns the Forests of the Midwest?

In monitoring forest ownership, we distinguished between public (National Forest, other Federal, State, and local government) and private (industrial and non-industrial) ownership of timberland. We calculated change in the area of timberland in private ownership.

Growing-Stock Volume, Growth, Removals, and Timber Products

For an excellent discussion of changes in the volume of growing-stock trees on timberland, tree growth and removals, and the production of timber products, please refer to *The Status of Timber Resources in the North Central United States*, a publication of the North Central Research Station Forest Productivity Integrated Research Program; the document can be downloaded from our Web site at www.ncrs.fs.fed.us or a bound copy can be ordered by requesting Gen. Tech. Rep. NC-228.

How Has the Area of Forest Changed?

We calculated change in the total area of forest, and the area of forest in each of the dominant forest type groups in the region. Forest type and forest type groups are terms used to describe forests based on species composition. The Forest Inventory and Analysis research unit defines forest type as a classification of forest land in which the named species, either singly or in combination, makes up a plurality of live tree stocking. These types are based on a standard set of local forest types in the Forest Service Handbook and have been logically organized into broader forest type groups to facilitate reporting. So, how has the area of forest changed? We suspect that the answer will likely surprise many people.

Area of Forest: 1980

In 1980, there were 71.8 million acres of forest in the region, approximately 27 percent of the total land area (figures 19 and 20). At that time, nearly 70 percent of all forested land in the region occurred in the northern tier of the Lake States. The southern tier of Missouri, Illinois, and Indiana was also heavily forested (figure 21, 1980).

The answer will likely surprise many people. Region wide, the area of forest increased by 7 percent. At the State level, change in the area of forest ranged from an increase of 62,000 acres in Indiana to increases of more than 1.1 million acres in Minnesota and Missouri.

Percent of Land in Forest

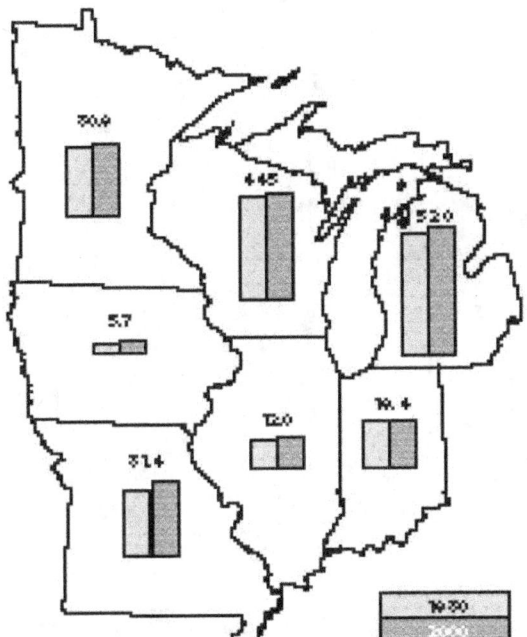

Figure 19. Percent of total land area classified as forest, 1980 and 2000. Values correspond with the year in which forest comprised the greater proportion of the total land area. Data source: USDA Forest Service FIADB.

Area of Forest
(million acres)

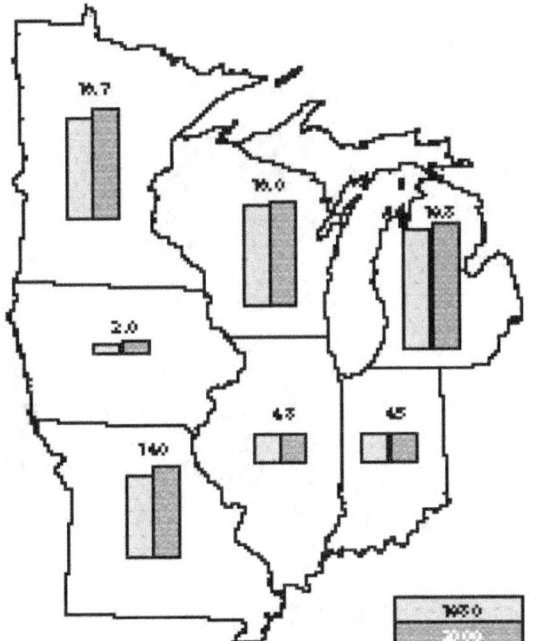

Figure 20. Area of land classified as forest (million acres), 1980 and 2000. Values correspond with the year that had the greater amount of forest. Data source: USDA Forest Service FIADB.

Area of Forest: 2000

In 2000, there were 76.8 million acres of forest in the region, and forest comprised approximately 30 percent of the total land area (figures 19 and 20). Once again most of the forests in the region occurred in the Lake States, and to a lesser degree in southern Missouri and Indiana (figure 21, 2000).

Percent Change: 1980 – 2000

At the county level, change in the total area of forest ranged from a decrease of 91 percent to an increase of 896 percent (figure 21, Change). "Hotspots" of change were most prevalent in southwestern Minnesota and central Iowa, and were the result of increases in the Oak/Hickory and Elm/Ash/Cottonwood forest type groups.

Interpreting Change in the Area of Forest

Region wide, the area of forest increased by 7 percent between 1980 and 2000. At the State level, percent change in the area of forest ranged from an increase of 1.4 percent in Indiana to an increase of 41 percent in Iowa (figure 22). In absolute terms, change in the area of forest ranged from an increase of 62,000 acres in Indiana to increases of more than 1.1 million acres in Minnesota and Missouri. To put this into perspective, consider that the annual increase in the total area of forest in Missouri was more than 96,000 acres, which is the equivalent of adding roughly 150 square miles of forest per year (figure 23).

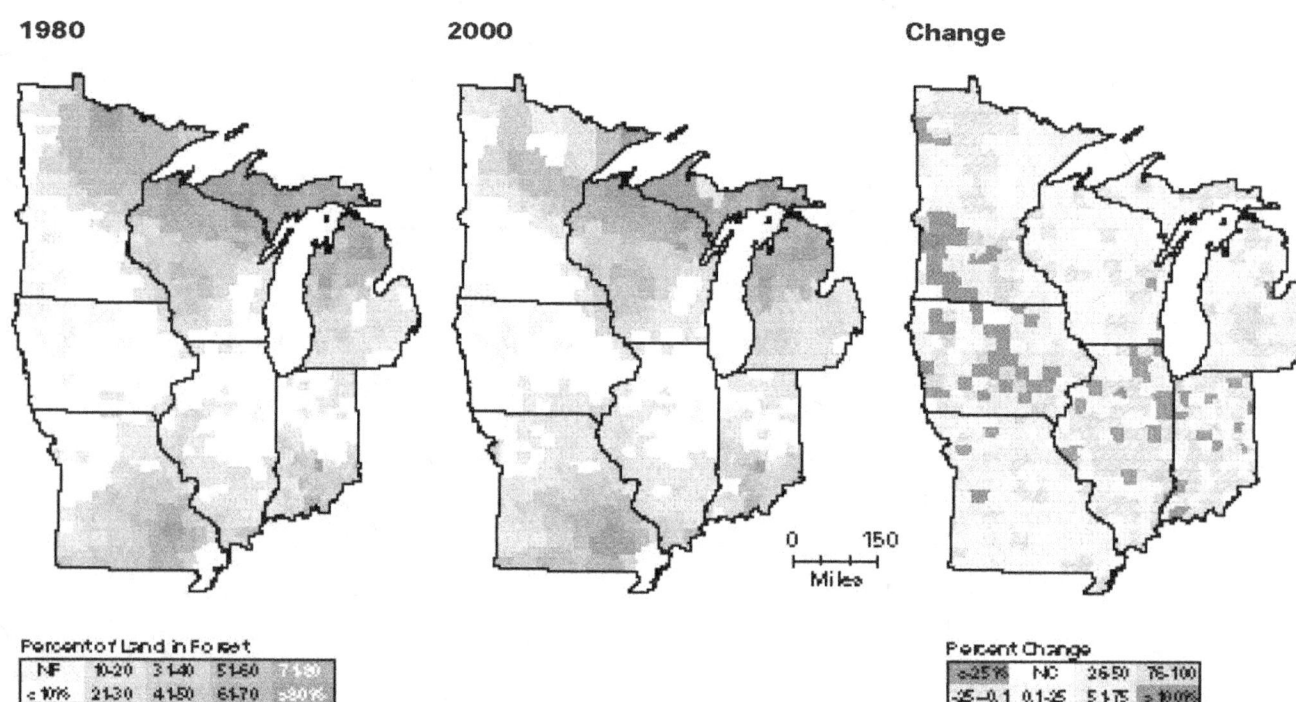

1980   **2000**   **Change**

Figure 21. Percent of total county land area classified as forest, 1980 and 2000. NF denotes counties with no forest. Percent change in county land area classified as forest, 1980-2000. Data source: USDA Forest Service FIADB.

22

Comparing Changes in Forestland and Forest

As noted in the Section introduction, *forestland* is a type of *land cover* and *forest* is a type of *land use*. The forestland land cover type describes land that is dominated by trees. As a rule of thumb, a canopy closure or aerial crown density of at least 40 percent is required before a tract of land will be classified as forestland. Forestland is generally monitored remotely via aerial photography or satellite imagery. Forest, alternatively referred to as forest land or forested land, is land that is at least 10 percent stocked by forest trees of any size, or formerly having had such tree cover, and not currently developed for nonforest use. The minimum area for classification of forest land is 1 acre. Forest is generally monitored via on-the-ground field sampling.

Although forestland and forest are not the same, some measures of the two were similar. In particular, note similarities in the percent of land classified as forestland (figure 7) and the percent of land classified as forest (figure 19). Also, note similarities in the area of forestland (figure 8) and the area of forest (figure 20).

Close inspection of the data reveals that the area of forestland is consistently less than the area of forest in areas that are lightly to moderately forested (i.e., Illinois, Indiana, and Iowa) and that the converse is true in heavily forested portions of the region (Michigan, Minnesota, Missouri, and Wisconsin). This trend is largely the result of the allocation procedure used to assign land cover class: When a land cover class could not be readily assigned to a tract of land, the allocation procedure took into account the

Percent Change

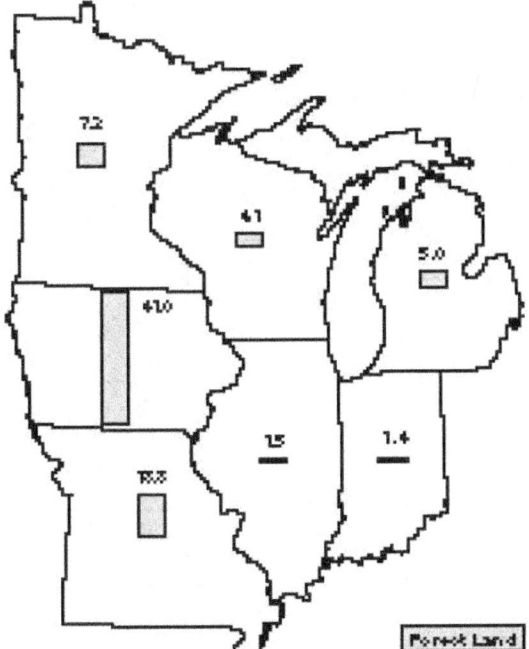

Figure 22. Percent change in area of land classified as forest, 1980-2000. Data source: USDA Forest Service FIADB.

Change (acres/year)

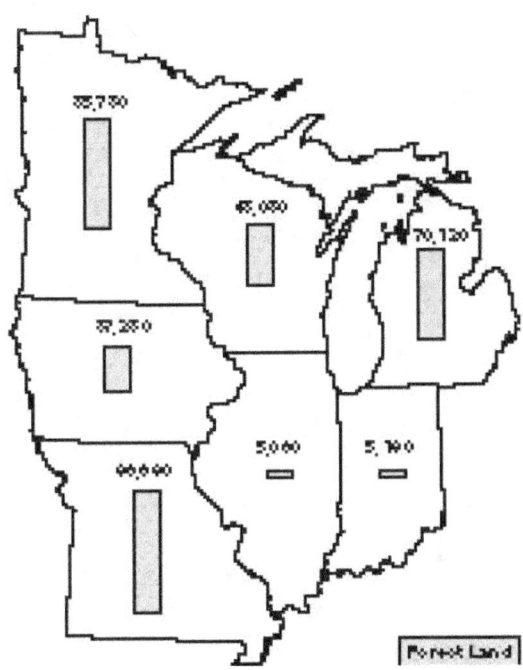

Figure 23. Annual change in area of land classified as forest (acres/year), 1980-2000. Data source: USDA Forest Service FIADB.

class of nearby tracts of land. Thus, a tract of uncertain status was more likely to be classified as forestland in heavily forested areas than in other areas.

The one exception that stands out is the difference between forestland and forest in Iowa. In Iowa, the area of forestland was estimated to have increased by 11.5 percent between 1980 and 2000, whereas the area of forest was estimated to have increased by 41 percent. In absolute terms, the area of forestland in Iowa increased by approximately 170,500 acres, whereas the area of forest increased by more than 595,000 acres. There are a number of plausible explanations for this difference. The most likely explanation is that the increases in forest occurred along the borders of streams, rivers, and fence lines in landscapes that were otherwise dominated by agriculture, and, even though the overall increase in the area of forest was substantial, on a tract-by-tract basis the increase was not sufficient to trigger a reclassification from the agriculture cover type to forestland.

How Has Forest Composition Changed?

Forest composition is a reference to the mix of tree species within a forest. In the Midwest, there are 125 species of forest trees. Each has been assigned to one or more of 28 forest type groups, which are comprised of species of trees that share similar characteristics and habitat requirements. For example, the Oak/Hickory forest type group is comprised of various species of oak and hickory trees commonly found growing together; a forest would be classified as Oak/Hickory if the plurality of trees were associated with the Oak/Hickory forest type group. We calculated change in the prevalence of the most common forest type groups in the region including Oak/Hickory, Maple/Beech/Birch, Aspen/Birch, Spruce/Fir, and Elm/Ash/Cottonwood.

Forest Composition: 1980

In order, the most prevalent forest type groups in the region were Oak/Hickory, Aspen/Birch, Maple/Beech/Birch, Spruce/Fir, and Elm/Ash/Cottonwood. Collectively, they accounted for over 90 percent of the total area of forest in the region. Oak/Hickory was dominant in Missouri, Indiana, and Illinois; Maple/Beech/Birch was dominant in Michigan, Wisconsin, and Iowa; and Aspen/Birch was dominant in Minnesota (figure 24).

Forest Composition: 2000

In order, Oak/Hickory, Maple/Beech/Birch, Aspen/Birch, Spruce/Fir, and Elm/Ash/Cottonwood were the most prevalent forest type groups in the region. Oak/Hickory was dominant in Missouri, Illinois, and Iowa; Maple/Beech/Birch was dominant in Michigan, Wisconsin, and Indiana; and Aspen/Birch was dominant in Minnesota (figure 25).

Region wide, the total area of forest increased by 5 million acres. Oak/Hickory remained the dominant forest type, but Maple/Beech/Birch increased by more than twice as much as any other forest type. Aspen/Birch and Spruce/Fir were the only major forest types to show a decline.

Forest Composition: 1980
(percent)

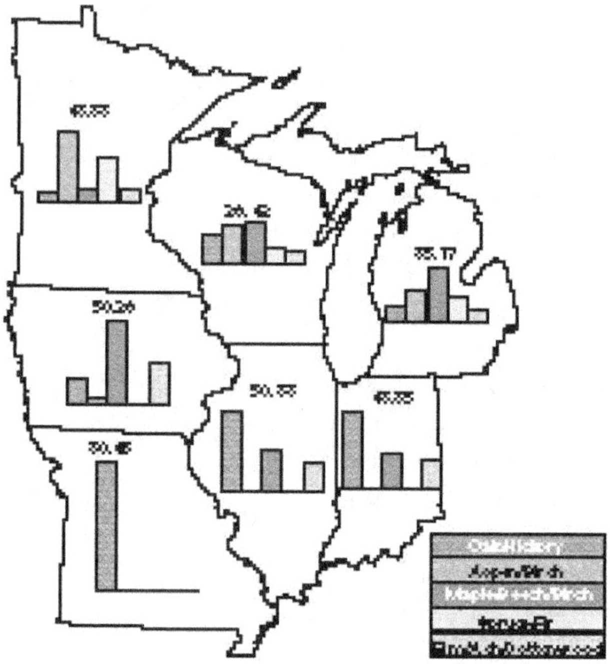

Forest Composition: 2000
(percent)

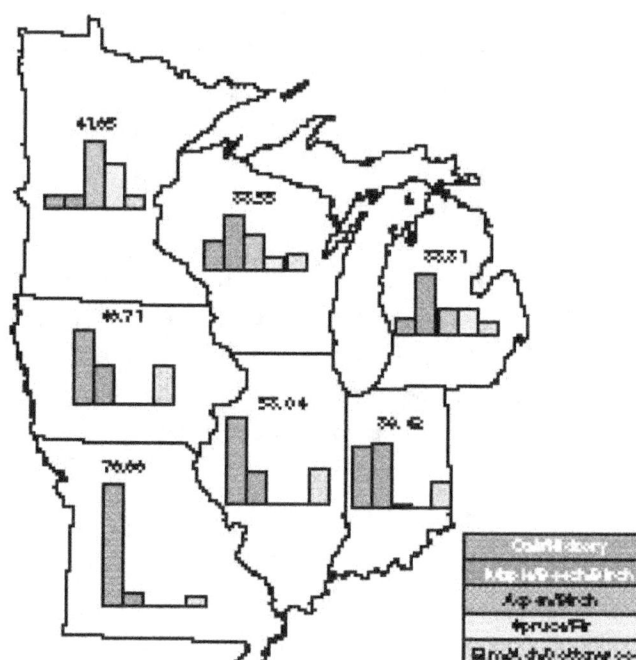

Figure 24. Percent of total forest classified in each of the dominant forest type groups in the region, 1980. Values correspond with the most prevalent forest type group. Data source: USDA Forest Service FIADB.

Figure 25. Percent of total forest classified in each of the dominant forest type groups in the region, 2000. Values correspond with the most prevalent forest type group. Data source: USDA Forest Service FIADB.

Change in Forest Composition

Region wide, the total area of forest increased by 5 million acres. Although Oak/Hickory remained the dominant forest type group, in absolute terms, Maple/Beech/Birch increased by more than twice as much as any other forest type. Aspen/Birch and Spruce/Fir were the only major forest types to show a decline.

At the county level, change in the prevalence of Oak/Hickory and Maple/Beech/Birch (figure 26) and Elm/Ash/Cottonwood (figure 27) were common; changes ranged from decreases of nearly 100 percent to increases of more than 1,300 percent. Conversely, the prevalence of Aspen/Birch and Spruce/Fir dominated landscapes remained the same or declined (figure 27).

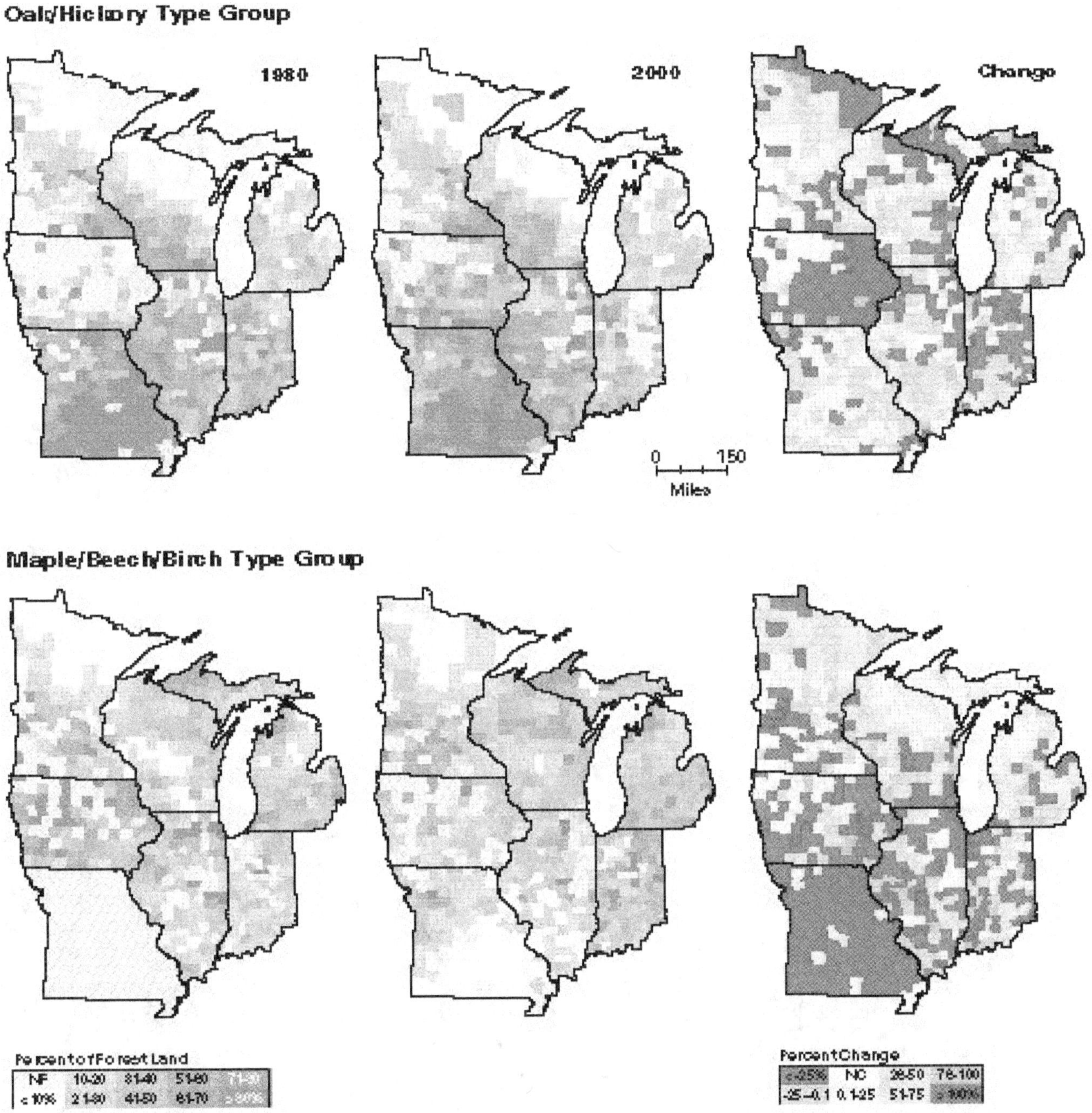

Oak/Hickory Type Group

Maple/Beech/Birch Type Group

Percent of Forest Land

NF	10-20	31-40	51-60	71-80
< 10%	21-30	41-50	61-70	> 80%

Percent Change

< -25%	NC	26-50	76-100
-25 – -0.1	0.1-25	51-75	> 100%

Figure 26. Percent of county forest land classified as Oak/Hickory or Maple/Beech/Birch in 1980 and 2000. NF indicates forest type group is not present. Percent change in area of forest classified as Oak/Hickory or Maple/Beech/Birch, 1980-2000. Data source: USDA Forest Service FIADB.

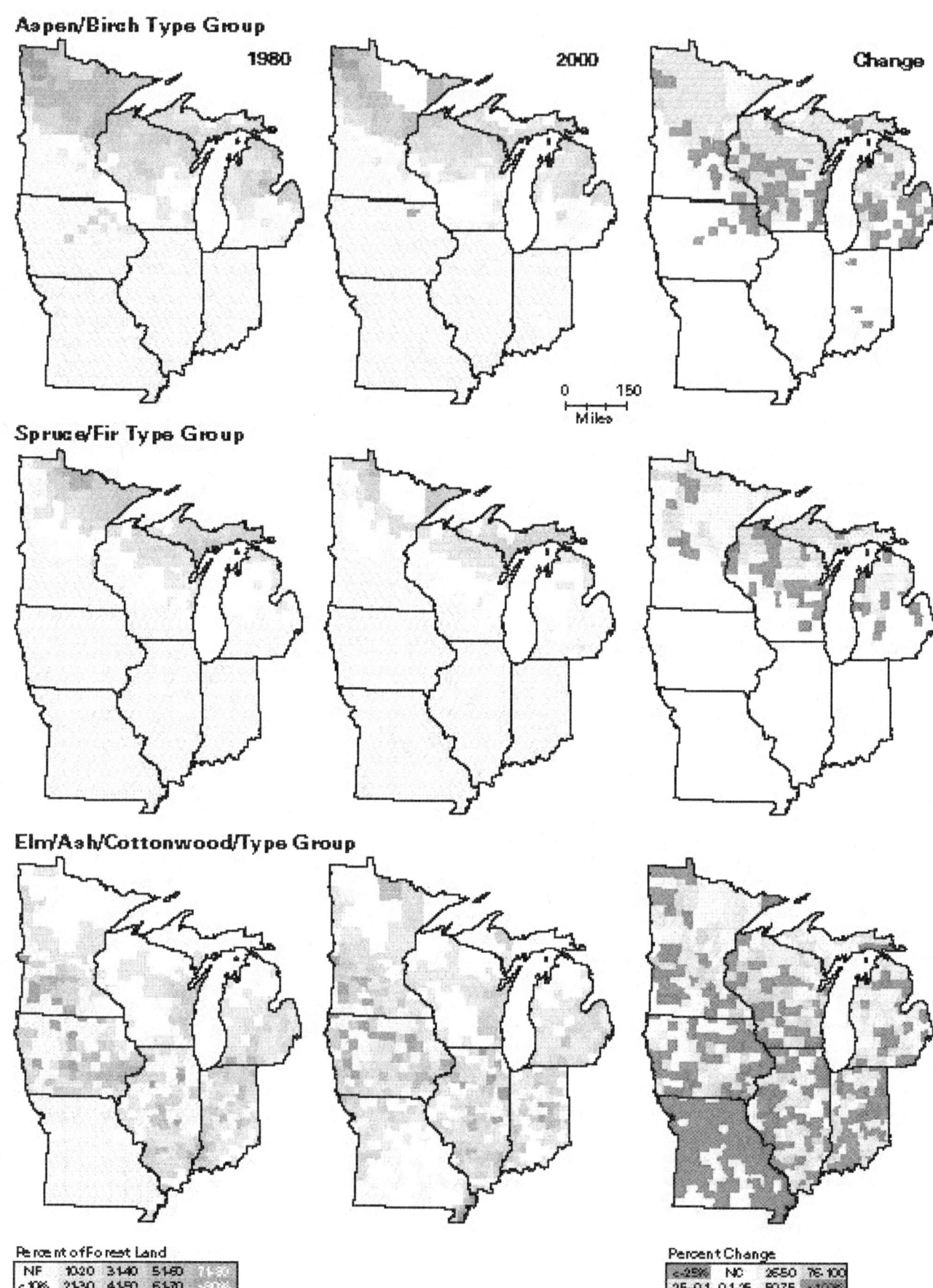

Aspen/Birch Type Group

1980   2000   Change

Spruce/Fir Type Group

Elm/Ash/Cottonwood/Type Group

Percent of Forest Land

NF	10-20	31-40	51-60	71-80
<10%	21-30	41-50	61-70	>80%

Percent Change

<-25%	NC	25-50	75-100
-25–0.1	0.1-25	50-75	>100%

Figure 27. Percent of county forest land classified as Aspen/Birch, Spruce/Fir, or Elm/Ash/Cottonwood in 1980 and 2000. NF indicates forest type group is not present. Percent change in area of forest classified as Aspen/Birch, Spruce/Fir, or Elm/Ash/Cottonwood, 1980-2000. Data source: USDA Forest Service FIADB.

Interpreting Changes in Forest Composition

At the State level, change in forest composition was most dramatic in Indiana and Missouri, involving Oak/Hickory and Maple/Beech/Birch forest type groups. In Indiana, the area of Maple/Beech/Birch increased by more than 750,000 acres, replacing Oak/Hickory as the most prevalent forest type in the State. In Missouri, Oak/Hickory remained the most prevalent forest type, but Maple/Beech/Birch increased by more than 1 million acres, replacing Elm/Ash/Cottonwood as the second most common forest type. Noteworthy changes also occurred in Michigan and Wisconsin, where the area of Aspen/Birch declined by more than 500,000 acres (table 1).

To put these changes into perspective, consider that the annual increase of Oak/Hickory forests in Missouri was nearly 47,000 acres (roughly 73 square miles) per year (figure 28). The annual loss of Aspen/Birch in Wisconsin was nearly 40,000 acres (approximately 62.5 square miles) per year (figure 29).

Table 1. Percent change (%) and absolute change (acres) in the area of forest by forest type group, 1980-2000. Data source: USDA Forest Service FIADB.

	Oak/ Hickory		Maple/ Beech/Birch		Aspen/ Birch		Spruce/Fir		Elm/Ash/Cottonwood	
	%	Acres	%	Acres	%	Acres	%	Acres	%	Acres
Illinois	6.9	148,519	-24.1	-269,661	0	0	0	0	24.0	180,384
Indiana	-23.0	-499,184	75.9	765,760	7.16×10^5	7,162	0	0	-21.4	-185,915
Iowa	320.0	729,600	-30.6	-223,800	-85.7	-43,800	0	0	38.9	145,300
Michigan	9.3	172,763	14.3	925,873	-13.9	-518,381	-1.8	-53,003	14.2	207,005
Minnesota	14.9	155,000	18.3	222,300	1.7	117,300	2.8	124,400	13.5	161,300
Missouri	7.9	792,800	1.01×10^8	1,012,999	0	0	0	0	3170.8	608,800
Wisconsin	0.3	8,599	32.2	1,303,256	-12.9	-517,854	-16.5	-268,081	16.9	222,533
Region	7.4	1,508,097	25.6	3,736,727	-6.5	-955,571	-2.2	-196,684	22.4	1,339,407

Annual Change
(acres/year)

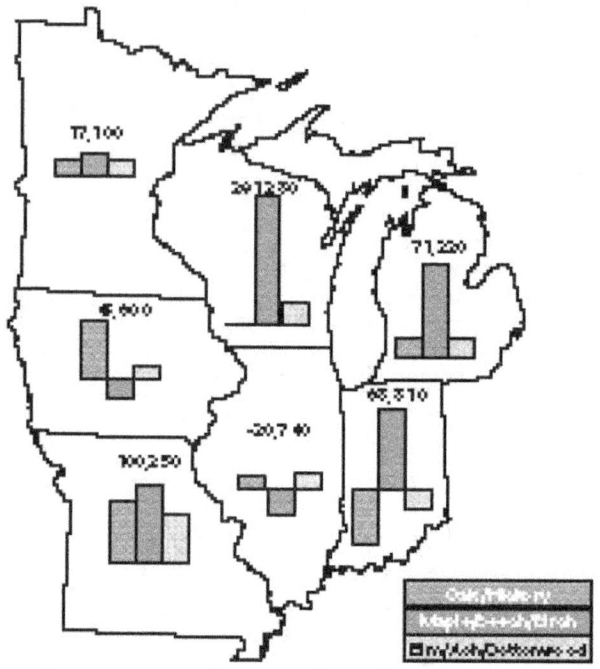

Figure 28. Annual change in area (acres/year) of forest by forest type group, 1980-2000. Values correspond with forest type group that changed the most. Data source: USDA Forest Service FIADB.

Annual Change
(acres/year)

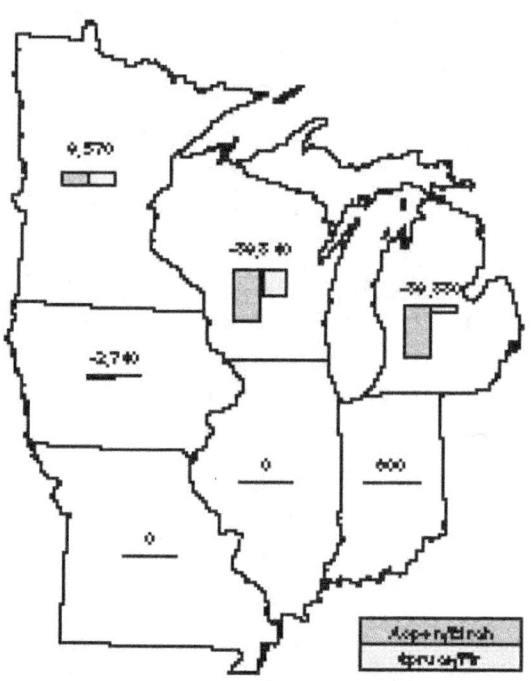

Figure 29. Annual change in area (acres/year) of forest by forest type group, 1980-2000. Values correspond with forest type group that changed the most. Data source: USDA Forest Service FIADB.

How Has Forest Structure Changed?

The structure of a forest has to do with the age, size, and spatial arrangement of the trees within. Understanding how the structure of forests has changed is vitally important, because, for many people, structure is what actually makes a forest a forest. Of course, the structure of a forest also has significant ecological and economic implications, but very often people remain ambivalent about change until the change is inconsistent with their vision of what a forest should look like.

The presence of big trees is a defining characteristic of a forest for many people. Therefore, we defined changes in forest structure in terms of stand size. The Forest Inventory and Analysis research unit defines stand size based on the ratio of large-, medium-, and small-diameter trees in a given stand, and recognizes three stand-size classes: large, medium, and small.

We calculated change in the prevalence of all three stand-size classes; however, given the widespread interest in big trees, maps are only presented for timberland that is dominated by large-diameter trees. Timberland is forested land that is producing, or is capable of producing, in excess of 20 cubic feet per acre per year of industrial roundwood products under natural conditions, is not withdrawn for timber utilization by stature or administrative regulation, and is not associated with urban or rural development.

Forest Structure: 1980

In 1980, there was 67.6 million acres of timberland in the region, the majority (41 percent) of which was stocked with medium-diameter trees. Of the remaining timberland, 36 percent was stocked with large-diameter trees, and 23 percent was stocked with small-diameter trees. At the county level, the amount of timberland dominated by large-diameter trees ranged from 5.6 percent to 100 percent (figure 30, 1980). Among the most common forest type groups in the region, the majority of large-diameter trees were Oak/Hickory or Maple/Beech/Birch; the majority of medium- and small-diameter trees were Aspen/Birch or Oak/Hickory (Appendix B).

Forest Structure: 2000

In 2000, there was 72.5 million acres of timberland in the region, the majority (44 percent) of which was stocked with large-diameter trees. Of the remaining timberland, 32 percent was stocked with medium-diameter trees, and 24 percent was stocked with small-diameter trees. At the county level, the amount of timberland dominated by large-diameter trees ranged from less than 1 percent to 100 percent (figure 30, 2000). The majority of large-diameter trees in the region were Oak/Hickory or Maple/Beech/Birch; the majority of medium-diameter trees were Maple/Beech/Birch or Oak/Hickory; and the majority of small-diameter trees were Oak/Hickory or Maple/Beech/Birch (Appendix B).

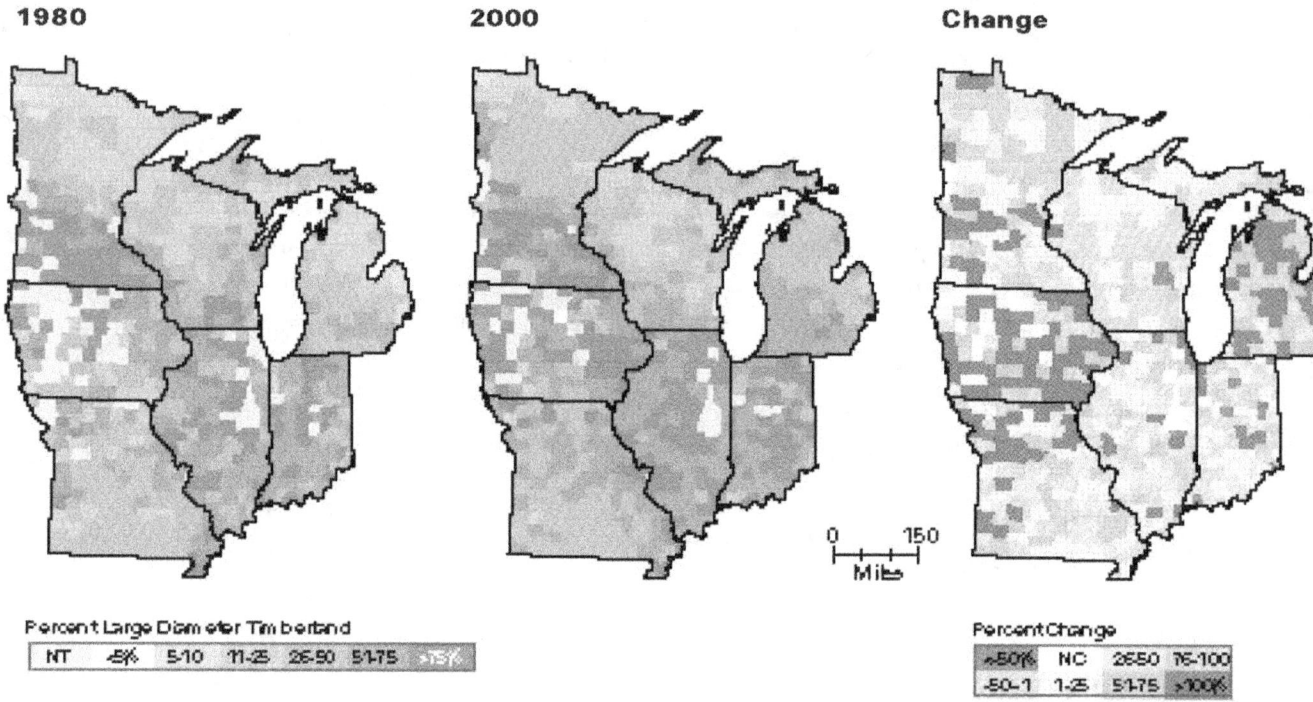

1980   **2000**   **Change**

Percent Large Diameter Timberland

| NT | <5% | 5-10 | 11-25 | 26-50 | 51-75 | >75% |

Percent Change

| <-50% | NC | 26-50 | 76-100 |
| -50–1 | 1-25 | 51-75 | >100% |

Figure 30. Percent of timberland classified as large diameter, 1980 and 2000. NT indicates no large-diameter timberland present. Percent change in area of large-diameter timberland, 1980-2000. Data source: USDA Forest Service FIADB.

Change in Forest Structure

At the county level, change in the prevalence of large-diameter timberland ranged from a decrease of 94.7 percent to an increase of more than 1,200 percent (figure 30, Change). To view maps that depict change in medium- and small-diameter timberland, view the Changing Midwest Web site at www.ncrs.fs.fed.us/4153/deltawest/ and select **Tree Size Class.**

How has the structure of midwestern forests changed? Region wide, the prevalence of large-diameter timberland increased by 30.2 percent; medium-diameter timberland decreased by 14.5 percent, and small-diameter timberland increased by 9.2 percent. In absolute terms, the greatest changes occurred in Michigan, where the total area of large-diameter timberland increased by more than 3.1 million acres, and the area of large-diameter Maple/Beech/Birch forests increased by more than 1 million acres.

Interpreting Change in Forest Structure: Large-Diameter Timberland

The prevalence of large-diameter timberland increased by 30.2 percent region wide. The prevalence of medium-diameter timberland decreased by 14.5 percent, and the prevalence of small-diameter timberland increased by 9.2 percent. Further, consider that the amount of large-diameter timberland increased in each of the States in the region, except Wisconsin, ranging from a loss of 4 percent in Wisconsin to an increase of 130 percent in Iowa (figure 31). In absolute terms, the greatest change occurred in Michigan, where the total area of large-diameter timberland increased by 3.1 million acres (figure 32). By forest type group, the greatest changes occurred in Michigan and Missouri, where large diameter Maple/Beech/Birch and Oak/Hickory, respectively, increased by more than 1 million acres (figure 33).

Interpreting Changes in Forest Structure: Medium-Diameter Timberland

The amount of medium-diameter timberland decreased in Iowa, Michigan, Minnesota, and Missouri. Percent change in medium-diameter timberland ranged from a loss of 31 percent in Iowa to an increase of 51 percent in Indiana. In absolute terms, the greatest changes occurred in Michigan, where the total area of medium-diameter timberland decreased by 1.9 million acres, and in Indiana, where medium-diameter timberland increased by 345,000 acres. By forest type group, the greatest changes occurred in Minnesota where Aspen/Birch declined by more than 1.4 million acres, and in Wisconsin where Maple/Beech/Birch increased by 715,500 acres (figure 33).

Percent Change

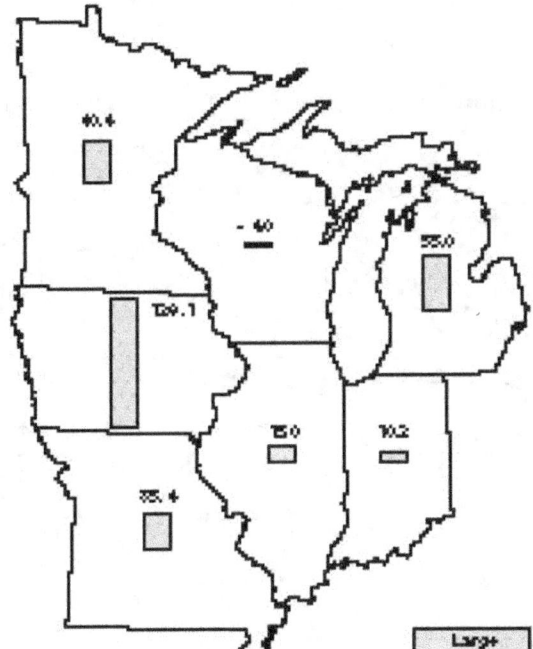

Figure 31. Percent change in area of large-diameter timberland, 1980-2000. Data source: USDA Forest Service FIADB.

Change
(thousand acres)

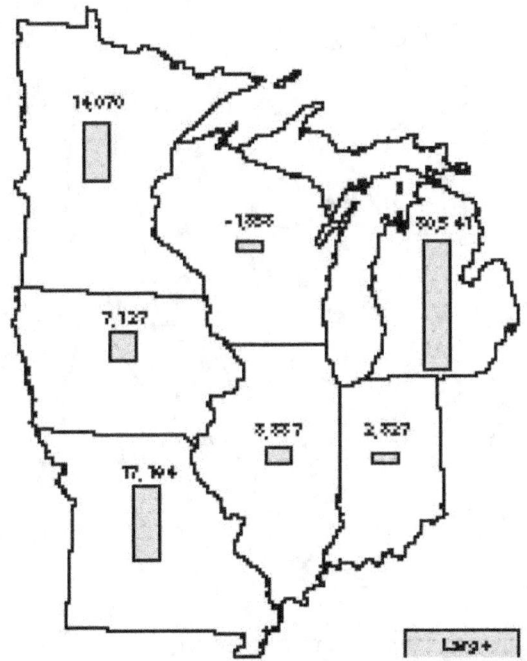

Figure 32. Change in area of large-diameter timberland (thousand acres), 1980-2000. Data source: USDA Forest Service FIADB.

Interpreting Changes in Forest Structure: Small-Diameter Timberland

The amount of small-diameter timberland decreased in Illinois, Indiana, and Iowa. Percent change in small-diameter timberland ranged from a loss of 82 percent in Illinois to an increase of 42 percent in Minnesota. In absolute terms, the greatest change occurred in Minnesota, where the area of small-diameter timberland increased by 1.3 million acres. By forest type group, the greatest changes occurred in Minnesota, where Aspen/Birch declined by nearly 1.2 million acres and Spruce/Fir increased by 418,200 acres (figure 33).

Annual Percent Change

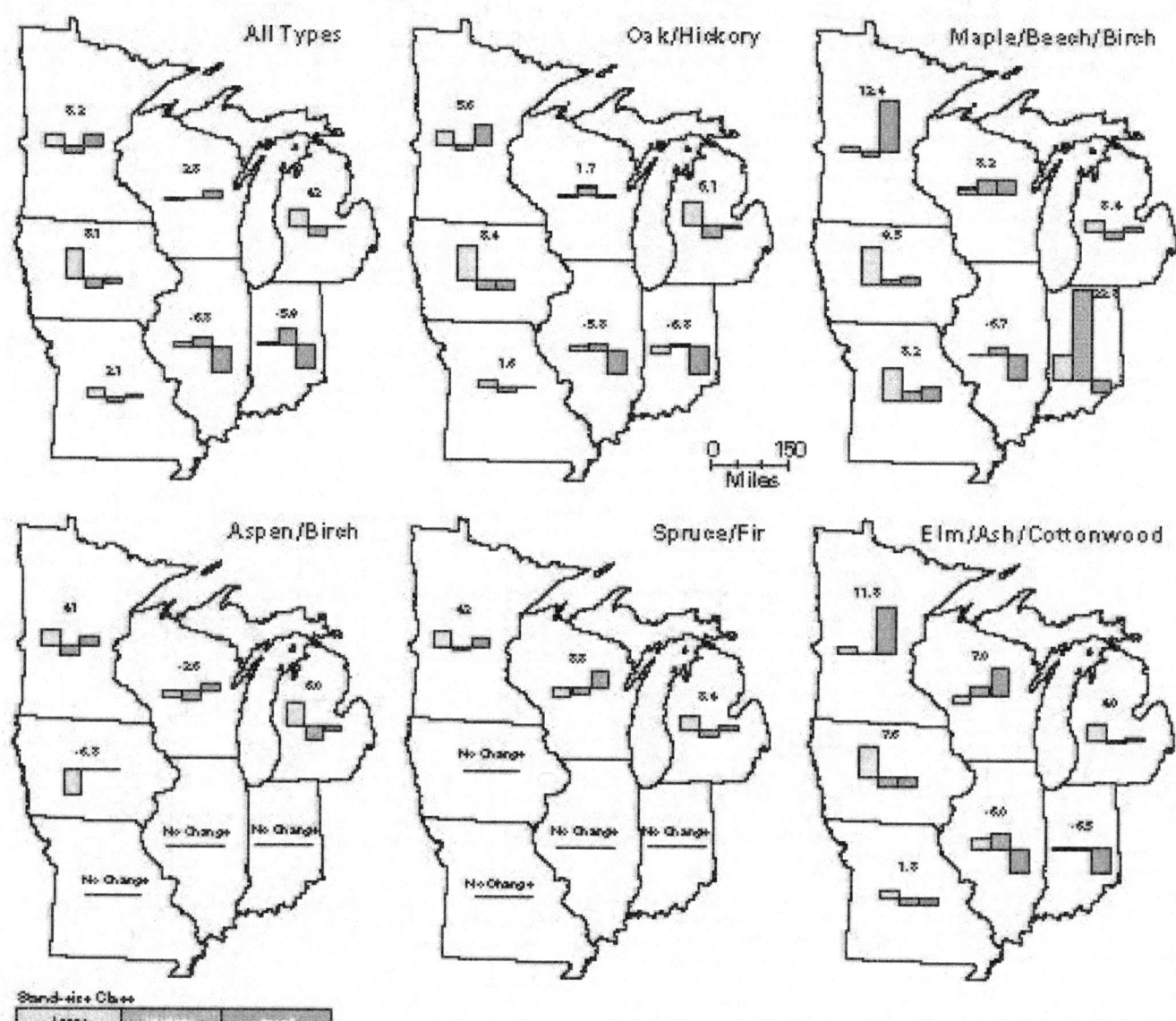

Figure 33. Percent change in area of large-, medium-, and small-diameter timberland by forest type group, 1980-2000. Value corresponds with size class that experienced the greatest change. Data source: USDA Forest Service FIADB.

How Has Timberland Ownership Changed?

In monitoring forest ownership, the Forest Inventory and Analysis research unit distinguishes between public and privately owned timberland. In assessing change in ownership, we concentrated on privately owned industrial and non-industrial timberland. Non-industrial status indicates that the landowner does not own or operate a primary wood-processing plant.

Understanding changes in the amount of timberland in private ownership, and distinguishing between industrial and non-industrial ownership, is critical for a number of reasons. First and foremost, the majority of timberland in the region is privately owned. Further, given that public and private timberlands are often in close proximity, the management that occurs on privately owned timberland often has impacts on publicly owned timberland. Finally, distinguishing between industrial and non-industrial

timberland is important because these lands are typically managed differently, thereby resulting in different impact on public timberland.

Timberland Ownership: 1980

In 1980, approximately 69 percent of the 67.5 million acres of timberland in the region was privately owned. The majority of privately owned timberland (82.2 percent) was in private non-industrial ownership. At the county level, the prevalence of timberland in private ownership ranged from 0 to 100 percent (figure 34, 1980).

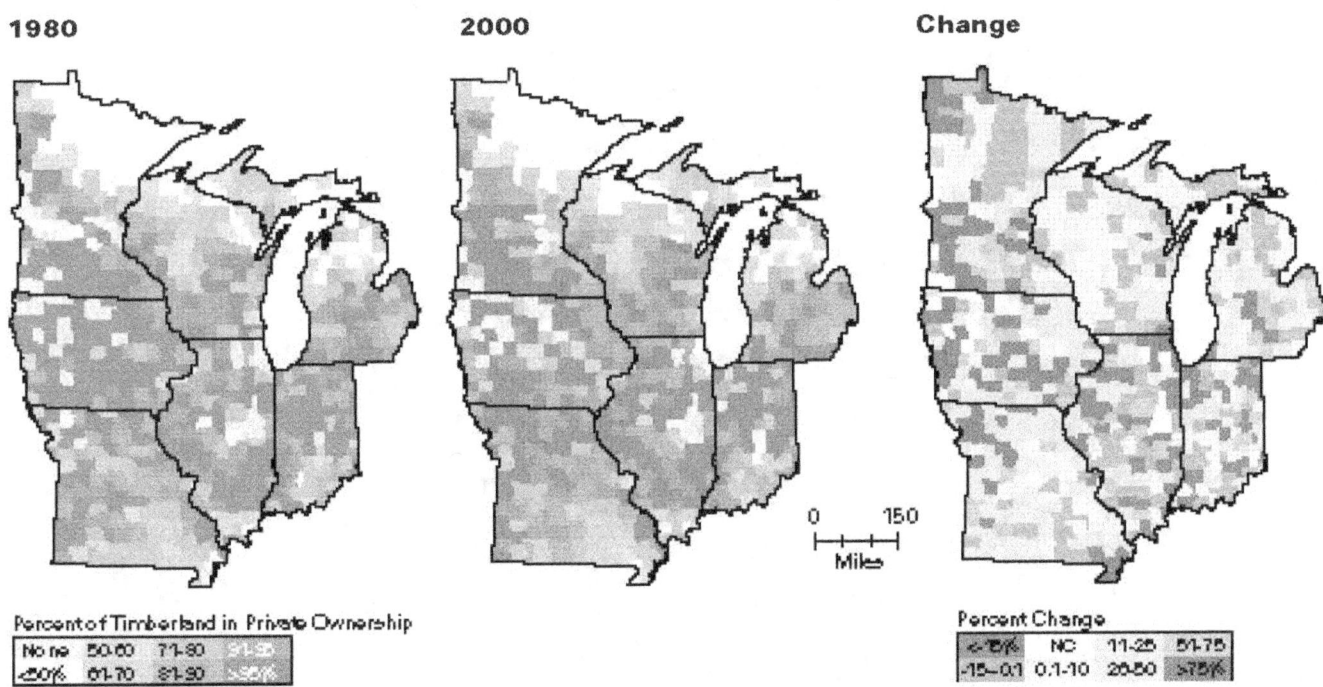

1980　　　　**2000**　　　　**Change**

Percent of Timberland in Private Ownership

| None | 50-60 | 71-80 | 91-99 |
| <50% | 61-70 | 81-90 | 100% |

Percent Change

| <-75% | NC | 11-25 | 51-75 |
| -75-0.1 | 0.1-10 | 26-50 | >75% |

Figure 34. Percent of timberland in private ownership, 1980 and 2000. Percent change in area of privately owned timberland, 1980-2000. Data source: USDA Forest Service FIADB.

Timberland Ownership: 2000

In 2000, approximately 69 percent of the 72.8 million acres of timberland in the region was privately owned. As was the case in 1980, the majority of privately owned timberland (82.6 percent) was in private non-industrial ownership. At the county level, the prevalence of timberland in private ownership ranged from 0 to 100 percent (figure 34, 2000).

Change in Timberland Ownership

At the county level, change in the prevalence of privately owned timberland ranged from a decrease of 91 percent to an increase of 831 percent (figure 34, Change). It is important to note that changes in private ownership do not necessarily mean that public timberlands were bought or sold; some of the changes were administrative or physical. For example, privately held agricultural lands that naturally reverted to forest, or were intentionally converted, would have been reclassified as timberland, assuming harvest was permissible.

Interpreting Changes in Ownership

Region wide, the amount of timberland in private ownership increased by 7.5 percent, from 46.5 million acres in 1980 to 50.0 million acres in 2000. At the State level, change in the prevalence of private industrial timberland ranged from a decrease of less than 1 percent in Indiana to an increase of 26 percent in Iowa. Change in the prevalence of private non-industrial timberland ranged from a decrease of 5.4 percent in Indiana to an increase of 213 percent in Iowa (figure 35).

To put this into perspective, consider that annual change in the area of private industrial timberland ranged from a decrease of more than 2,100 acres in Wisconsin to an increase of more than 11,000 acres in Missouri; annual change in the area of non-industrial timberland ranged from a decrease of nearly 1,600 acres in Indiana to an increase of more than 68,500 acres in Missouri (figure 36).

Who owns the forests of the Midwest?

The majority of timberland in the region is in private, non-industrial ownership. At the county level, no less than 82 percent of privately owned timberland was in non-industrial status. Non-industrial status indicates that the landowner does not own or operate a primary wood processing plant, which is defined to include commercial operations that originate the primary processing of wood on a regular and continuous basis, such as pulp or paper mills, sawmills, panel board mills, or post and pole mills.

Percent Change

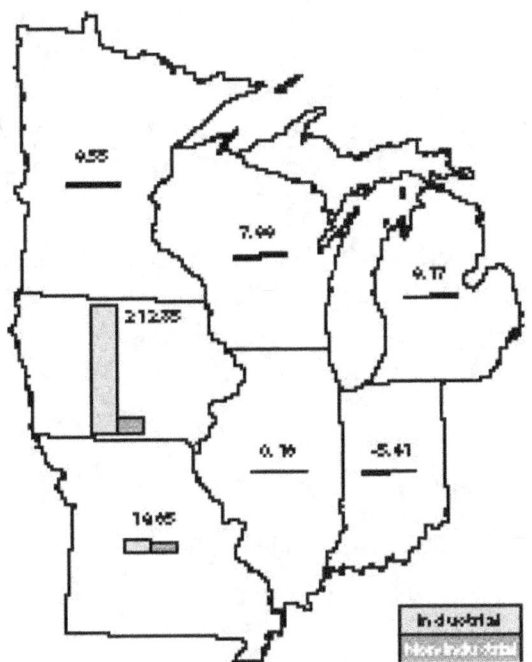

Figure 35. Percent change in the area of private industrial and private non-industrial timberland, 1980-2000. Data source: USDA Forest Service FIADB.

Change
(acres/year)

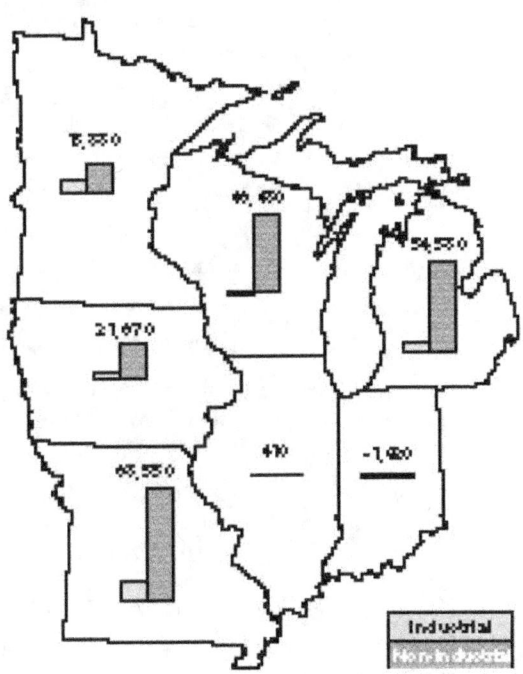

Figure 36. Annual change (acres/year) in the area of private industrial and private non-industrial timberland, 1980-2000. Data source: USDA Forest Service FIADB.

Introduction

Although the Forest Service does not have a comprehensive monitoring program for plants and animals on the scale of the Forest Inventory and Analysis program, our scientists are engaged in plant and wildlife research, and planners and managers carefully consider the impacts of forest management on plants and animals. We also work closely with Federal regulatory agencies and State resource management agencies to ensure that forests are managed with plants and animals in mind. In particular, we focus on threatened, endangered, and sensitive species and species of special concern that serve as indicators of forest health.

Currently, National Forest System lands in the Midwest provide critical habitat for 38 threatened and endangered species and 665 "Regional Forester Sensitive Species." To learn more about our Threatened, Endangered, and Sensitive Species Program and view the threatened and endangered and sensitive species lists, visit the USDA Forest Service Region 9 Web site at www.fs.fed.us/r9/wildlife/tes/index.html.

In assessing the impacts of landscape change on wildlife, we focused on white-tailed deer, and several species of birds.

White-tailed Deer

Although the white-tailed deer is not listed as a sensitive, threatened, or endangered species, it is a species of special concern for several reasons.

First, the recent discovery of chronic wasting disease (CWD) in the Midwest, and the likelihood that landscape change is contributing to the spread of CWD, has resulted in heightened awareness. Chronic wasting disease of the deer family is a transmissible spongiform encephalopathy (TSE), a member of infectious diseases, including scrapie (found in sheep), "mad cow" disease, and Creutzfeldt-Jakob Disease (found in humans), that affect animals and people (Laplanche et al. 1999). Chronic wasting disease in deer is characterized by weight loss, behavioral changes, polydypsia, polyuria, and hypersalivation; it invariably results in death.

The size of the deer population is also of concern because of deer-car collisions, and the negative impact overbrowsing can have on manicured lawns and the habitat of birds and other animals (Alverson et al. 1988).

In order to monitor changes in white-tailed deer populations, we utilized annual harvest statistics that are collected by State resource management agencies. Harvest statistics are collected at the county level in each of the Midwestern States, with the exception of Michigan, which collects and summarizes data for Deer Management Areas. Here we answer the question: How have seasonal housing, game farms, and deer harvest changed? Change in total harvest intensity is depicted. Change in the harvest of antlered deer is depicted on the Changing Midwest Web site at www.ncrs.fs.fed.us/4153/deltawest/.

Birds

Many species of birds that live or breed in the Midwest are threatened, endangered, or sensitive, with, in many cases, the habitat they depend on being lost to development or browsing by deer. Not all bird species, however, respond negatively to development.

We considered two criteria in selecting species that we would monitor. First, we selected at least one species that lives and/or breeds in each of the major habitat types represented in the region (urban/early successional, grassland, and forest). Second, we selected species that are common and/or readily recognizable. We monitored population trends for the northern cardinal, Henslow's sparrow, and wood thrush. Population trends for other species are documented on the USDA Forest Service Changing Midwest Web site at www.ncrs.fs.fed.us/4153/deltawest/plantanimal/birds.

Data were retrieved from the United States Geological Survey (USGS) North American Breeding Bird Survey (www.mbr-pwrc.usgs.gov/bbs/intro00.html). Data analysis was conducted by John R. Sauer, Research Wildlife Biologist, USGS Patuxent Wildlife Research Center (www.pwrc.usgs.gov/) and Frank Thompson, Research Wildlife Biologist, USDA Forest Service North Central Research Station (www.ncrs.fs.fed.us/contact/profile/?id=219).

How Have Seasonal Housing, Game Farms, and Deer Harvest Changed?

The white-tailed deer is an important part of the cultural, economic, and biophysical landscapes of the Midwest. It is the designated or proposed State animal in Illinois, Michigan, Minnesota, and Wisconsin; the most abundant and sought after big-game animal in the region; and the main reason hunters contribute more than $3 billion to the economy of the Midwest each year.

Managing the biophysical landscape has always been an important part of deer management, and, given the discovery of CWD in Wisconsin in 2002, understanding landscape change is more important than ever because transmission appears to be lateral (Williams and Young 1992, Miller et al. 1998), suggesting that habitat fragmentation could increase the rate of and influence the direction of spread (Pelij 2002). Specifically, the perforation, compression, and fragmentation of habitat has the potential of decreasing the availability of suitable habitat, thereby increasing deer density, without reducing the potential for movement of infected animals among distinct populations (Gross and Miller 2001). In addition, it is important to note that CWD is unique among TSEs in that it is more prevalent in captive populations than in free ranging populations (Williams and Young

1980), suggesting that game farms may play an important role in the spread of CWD.

To better understand the relationship between landscape change, white-tailed deer, and CWD, we mapped percent change in seasonal housing and game farms, two significant forms of landscape change in the area of Wisconsin where CWD has been identified. We also mapped percent change in the harvest intensity of white-tailed deer across the region, which serves as an indicator of the size of the deer herd.

Seasonal Housing and Game Farms: 1980-2002

Although the CWD management zone in Wisconsin is limited to Dane, Sauk, and Iowa Counties, we mapped change in game farms and seasonal housing across most of the southern half of the State, given that the disease has been identified as far north as Portage County, and as far south as Winnebago and McHenry Counties in Illinois (Craven 2002). Within this 26-county zone, change in the number of game farms ranged from 0 percent in Green County to an increase of 1,000 percent in Waushara County (figure 37A). In absolute terms, the largest increase occurred in Portage County,

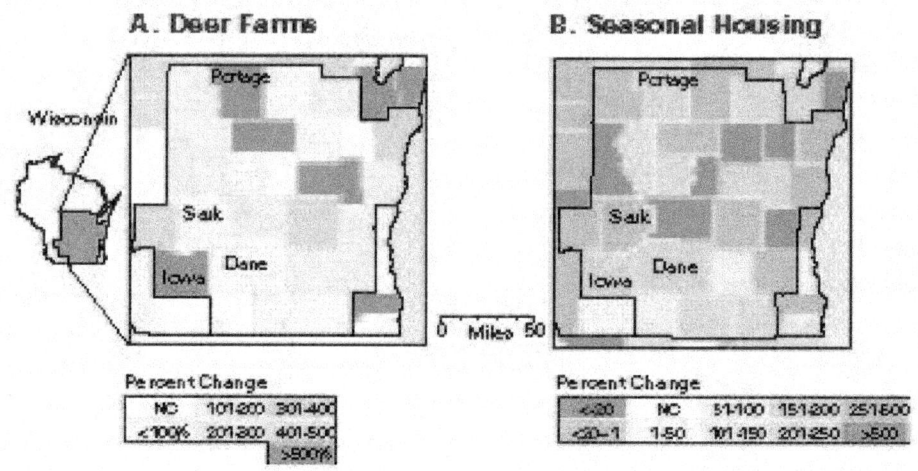

Figure 37. Percent change in the number of licensed deer farms (A) and seasonal housing units (B) within and around the CWD management zone in southern Wisconsin, 1980-2000. Data source: Wisconsin Department of Natural Resources Customer Service and Licensing (A); U.S. Census Bureau (B)

where there were 5 game farms in 1980 and 31 in 2002. Percent change in the number of seasonal housing units ranged from an increase of 60 percent in Green County to more than 1,500 percent in Calumet County (figure 37B).

Total Deer Harvest: 1980

Well over 550,000 white-tailed deer were harvested in the region in 1980. At the county level, harvest intensity (number of deer harvested per square mile) ranged from less than 1 deer per square mile to 12 deer per square mile (figure 38, 1980). Note: Michigan compiles harvest statistics by region, rather than by county. In 1980, there were three regions in Michigan.

Total Deer Harvest: 2000

Nearly 2 million white-tailed deer were harvested in the region in 2000. At the county level, harvest intensity ranged from less than 1 deer per square mile to more than 20 deer per square mile (figure 38, 2000).

Managing the biophysical landscape has always been an important part of deer management, and, given the discovery of CWD in Wisconsin in 2002, understanding landscape change is more important than ever. Within the endemic zone, change in the number of game farms ranged from 0 percent in Green County to 1,000 percent in Waushara County. Percent change in seasonal housing ranged from 60 percent in Green County to more than 1,500 percent in Calumet County.

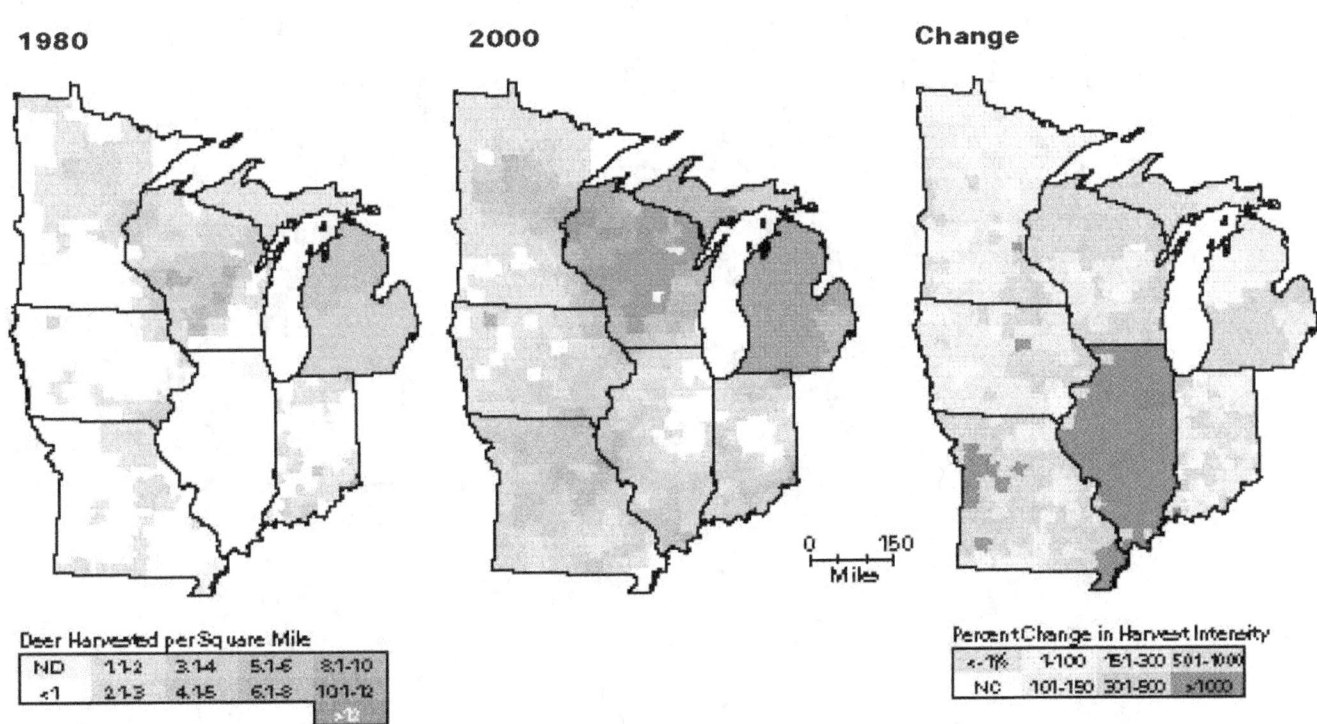

Figure 38. Total harvest intensity of white-tailed deer, 1980 and 2000. Percent change in harvest intensity, 1980-2000. ND indicates data were not available.

Change in Harvest Intensity

At the county level, percent change in harvest intensity ranged from a decrease of 45 percent to an increase of more than 19,500 percent in Ramsey County, Minnesota (figure 38, Change), which, in absolute terms, is an increase from 0.01 to 2.32 deer per square mile.

Interpreting Change in Harvest Intensity

Total harvest in the region increased by nearly 250 percent between 1980 and 2000. At the State level, annual change in the total number of deer harvested ranged from a 6-percent increase in Minnesota to a nearly 95-percent increase in Illinois (figure 39). In absolute terms, annual change in harvest intensity ranged from an increase of 4 deer per square mile in Indiana to an increase of nearly 23 deer per square mile in Wisconsin (figure 40).

Percent Change
(annual)

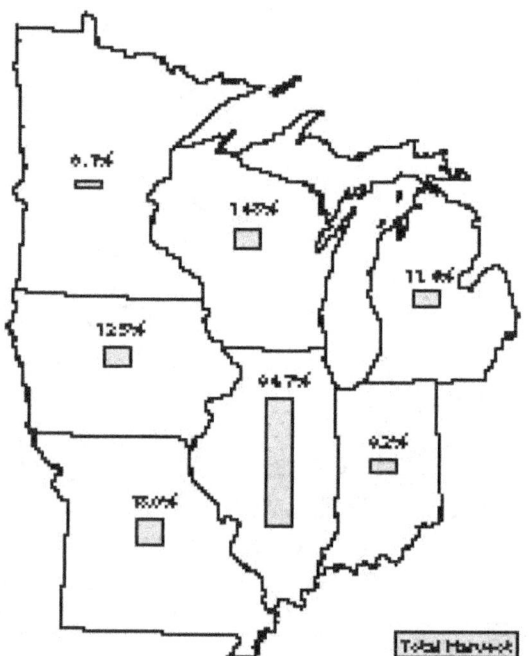

Figure 39. Percent annual change in total harvest intensity of white-tailed deer, 1980-2000.

Harvest Intensity
(deer/square mile/year)

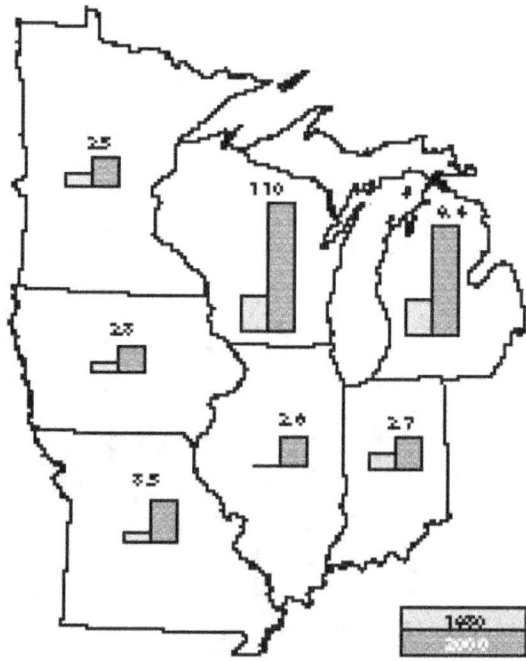

Figure 40. Annual change in total harvest intensity of white-tailed de 1980-2000.

Are Harvest Levels Appropriate?

Even without the added concern of CWD, one of the most difficult aspects of managing white-tailed deer is setting population goals and establishing harvest levels that are ecologically sustainable and socially acceptable. Although it is not our place to suggest whether or not wildlife managers have gotten it "right", we believe that managers in Wisconsin have done an excellent job of addressing the ecological and social sides of the equation. Further, it is our job to provide people with information they can use to determine whether or not wildlife managers are getting it right. It is important for people to know that deer populations within and surrounding the CWD management zone in Wisconsin generally exceed current population goals (figure 41), that hunting is the primary tool used to achieve population goals, and that failure to control the deer population could contribute to the spread of CWD.

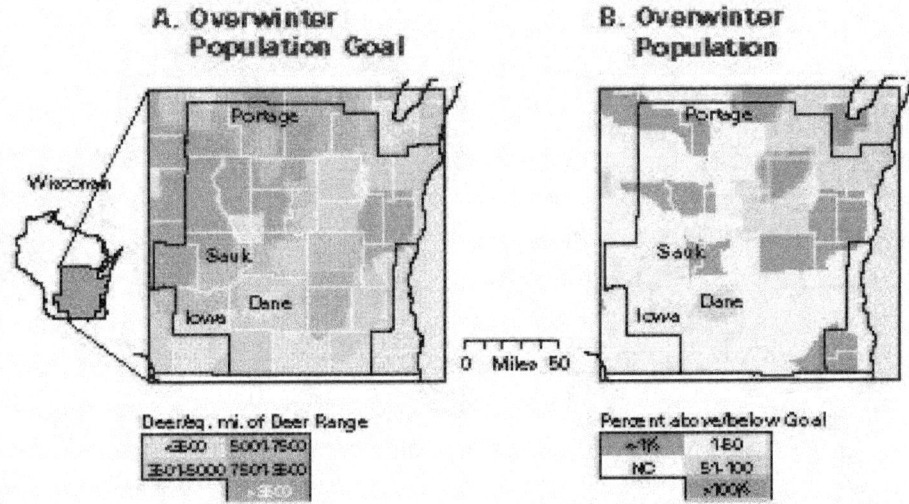

Figure 41. These maps indicate that the 2001 overwinter population goals within and surrounding the CWD management zone were not met. In general, the actual overwinter population exceeded the overwinter population goal. NC indicates no change. Data source: Wisconsin Department of Natural Resources.

How Have Bird Populations Changed?

Birds are important cultural symbols, and they enrich our lives in tangible ways. Collectively, Americans spend millions of days and billions of dollars pursuing bird-related recreation each year. To grasp how significantly birds contribute to our daily lives, and to the economy, consider that "birders" outnumber anglers by nearly 2:1 and hunters by more than 4:1 (table 2).

And, beyond simply enjoying birds, there is a growing recognition and appreciation of their ecological significance, and a growing willingness to protect sensitive, threatened, and endangered species. The Forest Service has initiated conservation assessments for 30 of the 38 species in the Midwest that are listed on the Regional Forester Sensitive Species list. To learn more about conservation assessments and the Forest Service Threatened, Endangered, and Sensitive Species Program, see www.fs.fed.us/r9/wildlife/tes. These efforts, and many others, are good news given that the relative abundance of a growing number of species is declining.

Evaluating Trends in Bird Populations

To assess changes in bird populations, we estimated the relative abundance of the northern cardinal (Cardinalis cardinalis), Henslow's sparrow (Ammodramus henslowii), and wood thrush (Hylocichla mustelina) over time using USGS Breeding Bird Survey data (Sauer et al. 2003).

Relative abundance is a measure of the average number of birds that an advanced birder would be expected to see in about 2.5 hours of birdwatching along roadsides. These species were selected because they live and or breed in each of the major habitat types in the region, including the urban/early successional, grassland, and forest habitat types. Further, each species is common or readily recognizable.

Briefly, we performed a poisson regression with log links on count data to estimate a single trend for each species. Observer data were used as covariates to account for the fact that different observers see and hear birds at varying levels of competence. The first year's data were eliminated for each observer to minimize the bias associated with start-up effect.

Route-level species trend estimates were used to develop grids representing relative abundance and percent change in relative abundance. In creating relative abundance grids we calculated the mean number of observations of each species for historical (1967-1971) and current (1996-2000) time periods. We interpolated from the center point of each route, using points that had at least 3 years of survey data during each time period. The resulting data were tested for global trends. For data sets with significant trends ($\alpha = 0.05$) we used universal kriging with a linear trend function. Finally, mean relative abundance values less than 0.1 were reclassified

Table 2. Comparison of the number of participants and rate of participation in consumptive and non-consumptive wildlife related recreation activities, 1980 and 1996. As reported in Caudill and Laughland (1998).

	1980		1996	
	Number of Participants (12 years and older)	**Proportion of Population**	**Number of Participants (16 years and older)**	**Proportion of Population**
Angling	59,354,000	32	35,246,000	17
Hunting	18,761,000	10	13,975,000	7
Wildlife Watching	121,125,000	66	62,868,000	31

to 0 to define species range. Maps were extracted within the boundaries of the seven Midwestern States. Maps depict relative abundance and percent change in relative abundance at a resolution of 1 km.

Relative Abundance of Northern Cardinal

The northern cardinal, a permanent resident, was selected to represent birds that breed in successional-scrub habitat. Identification and life history data are presented in Appendix C. Recall that estimates of relative abundance were based on actual Breeding Bird Survey (BBS) route-level observations that were averaged over 5 years, from 1967 to 1971 and from 1996 to 2001.

Relative Abundance: 1970

Route-level means of the number of cardinals detected during the BBS ranged from 0 to 101 in 1970, which means that on any given spring day a birder with advanced skills could reasonably have expected to see around 100 cardinals in about 2.5 hours of birdwatching along a BBS route that was in prime habitat. To see maps that depict route-level means, visit the Changing Midwest Web site at www.ncrs.fs.fed.us/4153/deltawest and select **Relative Abundance of Birds.** Our regional estimate of relative abundance ranged from 0 to 65 (figure 42, 1970).

Relative Abundance: 2000

Route-level means of the number of cardinals detected during the BBS ranged from 0 to 143 in 2000. Our regional estimate of relative abundance ranged from 0 to 47 (figure 42, 2000).

Change in Relative Abundance

Percent change of mean, route-level BBS observer data ranged from a decrease of 100 percent to an increase of 4,700 percent between 1970 and 2000. Our regional estimate of change in relative abundance ranged from a decrease of 100 percent to an increase of 1,919 percent (figure 42, Change).

1970   **2000**   **Change**

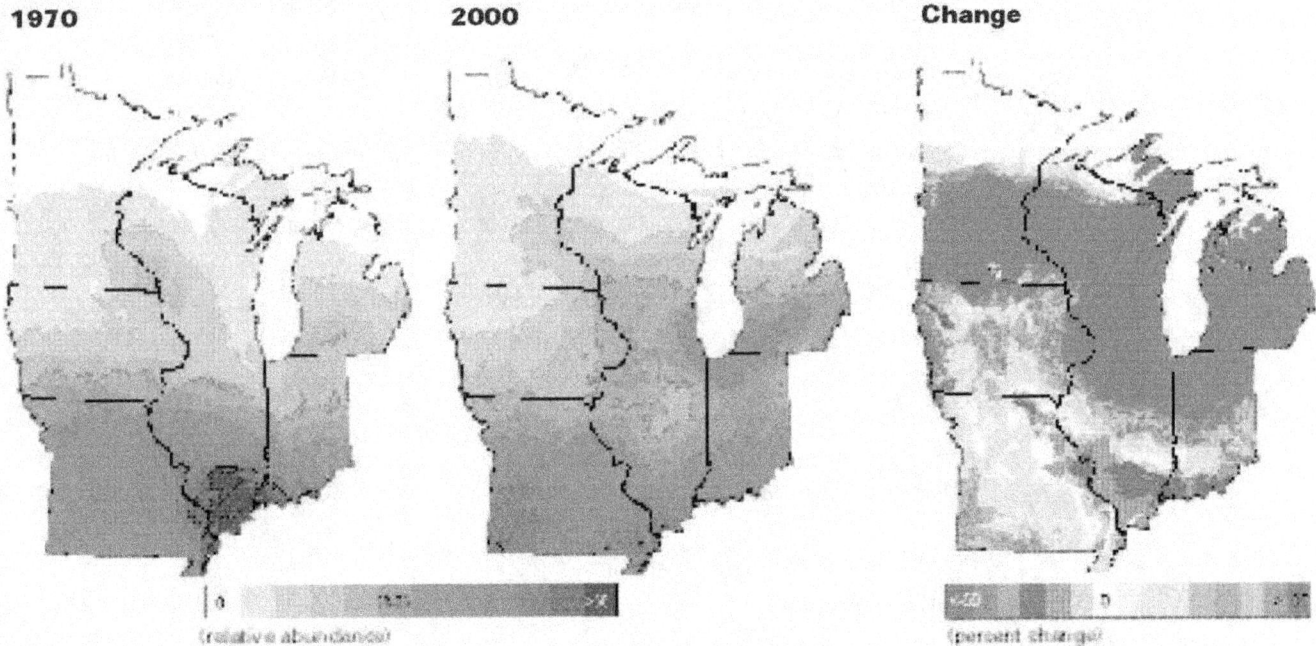

(relative abundance)   (percent change)

Figure 42. Estimated relative abundance of northern cardinal, 1970 and 2000. Percent change in relative abundance, 1970-2000. Data source: USGS Breeding Bird Survey.

Interpreting Change in Relative Abundance

Region wide, estimated relative abundance of the northern cardinal increased by 171 percent between 1970 and 2000. In absolute terms, the region-wide relative abundance of the northern cardinal increased from 13.6 to 15.0. In other words, in 1970 an advanced birder who spent 2.5 hours birdwatching at 10 random locations throughout the seven Midwestern States would have likely seen 136 northern cardinals. In 2000 that same birder would have likely seen 150 northern cardinals.

Relative Abundance of Henslow's Sparrow

Henslow's sparrow, a short distance migrant, was selected to represent birds that breed in grassland habitat. Identification and life history data are presented in Appendix C. Recall that estimates of relative abundance were based on actual Breeding Bird Survey (BBS) route-level observations that were averaged over 5 years, from 1967 to 1971 and from 1996 to 2001.

Relative Abundance: 1970

Route-level means of the number of Henslow's sparrows detected during the BBS ranged from 0 to 9, which means that on any given spring day in 1970 a birder with advanced skills could reasonably have expected to see around 9 Henslow's sparrows in about 2.5 hours of birdwatching along a BBS route that was in prime habitat. To see maps that depict route-level means, visit the Changing Midwest Web site at www.ncrs.fs.fed.us/4153/deltawest and select **Relative Abundance of Birds.** Our regional estimate of relative abundance (figure 43, 1970) ranged from 0 to 2. In other words, on any given spring day, a birder with advanced skills who spent 2.5 hours birdwatching along road-sides in Wisconsin (depicted in light green) could have reasonably expected to see about two Henslow's sparrows.

Relative Abundance: 2000

Route-level means of the number of Henslow's sparrows detected during the BBS ranged from 0 to 16 in 2000. Our regional estimate of relative abundance ranged from 0 to 6 (figure 43, 2000).

Change in Relative Abundance

Percent change of mean, route-level BBS observer data ranged from a decrease of 100 percent to an increase of 140 percent between 1970 and 2000. Our regional estimate of change in relative abundance ranged from a decrease of 84 percent to an increase of 556 percent (figure 43, Change).

Interpreting Change in Relative Abundance

Region wide, the estimated relative abundance of the Henslow's sparrow decreased by 7 percent between 1970 and 2000. In absolute terms, the region-wide relative abundance decreased from 0.15 to 0.03. In other words, in 1970 an advanced birder who spent 2.5 hours birdwatching at 100 random locations throughout the seven Midwestern States would have likely seen 15 Henslow's sparrows. In 2000, that same birder would have likely seen three.

Relative Abundance of Wood Thrush

The wood thrush, a neotropical migrant, was selected to represent birds that breed in woodland habitat. Identification and life history data are presented in Appendix C. Recall that estimates of relative abundance were based on actual Breeding Bird Survey (BBS) route-level observations that were averaged over 5 years, from 1967 to 1971 and from 1996 to 2001.

Relative Abundance: 1970

Route-level means of the number of wood thrush actually detected during the BBS ranged from 0 to 50, which means that on any given spring day in 1970 a birder with advanced skills could reasonably have expected to see around 50 wood thrushes in about 2.5 hours of birdwatching along a BBS route that was in prime habitat. To see maps that depict route-level means, visit the Changing Midwest Web site at www.ncrs.fs.fed.us/4153/deltawest and select **Relative Abundance of Birds.** Our regional estimate of relative abundance (figure 44, 1970) ranged from 0 to 9. In other words, on any given spring day, a birder with advanced skills who spent 2.5 hours birdwatching along roadsides in southern Indiana (depicted in bright green) could have reasonably expected to see about nine wood thrushes.

Relative Abundance: 2000

Route-level means of the number of wood thrush actually detected during the BBS ranged from 0 to 47 in 2000. Our regional estimate of relative abundance ranged from 0 to 10 (figure 44, 2000).

1970   **2000**   **Change**

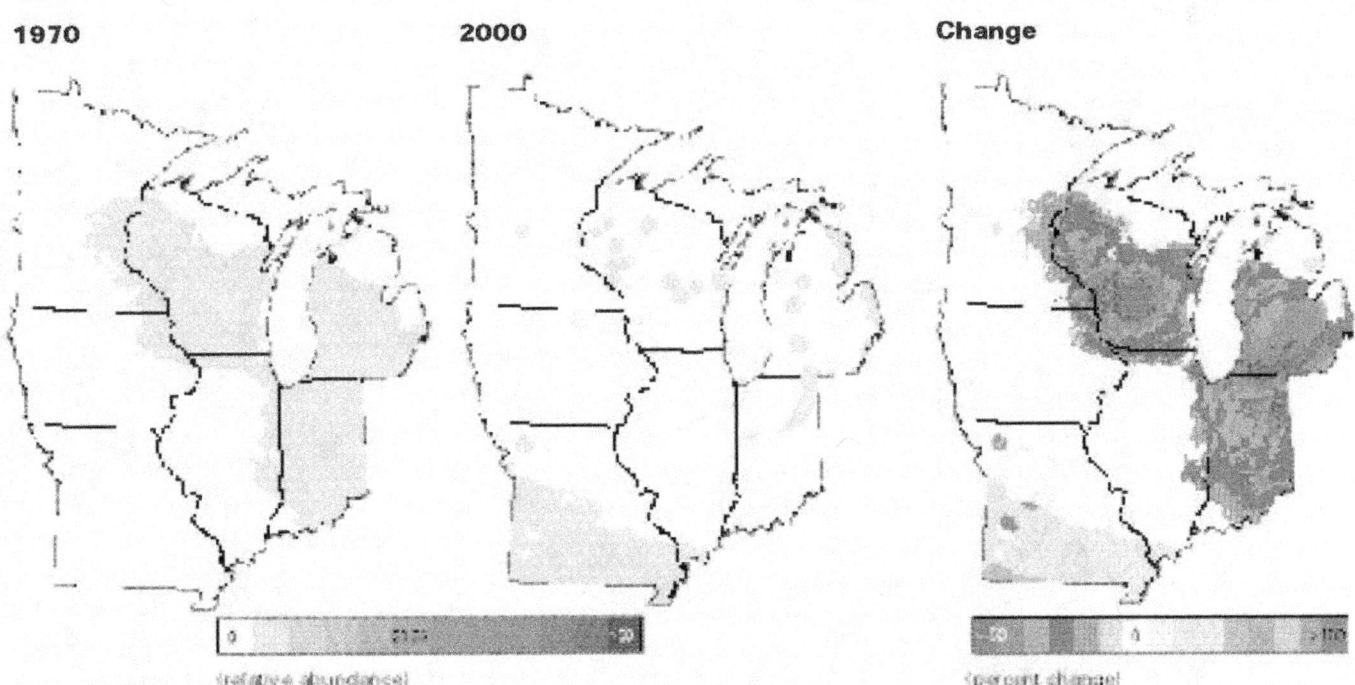

Figure 43. Estimated relative abundance of Henslow's sparrow, 1970 and 2000. Percent change in relative abundance, 1970-2000. Data source: USGS Breeding Bird Survey.

Change in Relative Abundance

Percent change of mean, route-level BBS observer data ranged from a decrease of 100 percent to an increase of 1,463 percent between 1970 and 2000. Our regional estimate of change in relative abundance ranged from a decrease of 100 percent to an increase of 950 percent (figure 44, Change).

Interpreting Change in Relative Abundance

Region wide, estimated relative abundance increased by 34 percent between 1970 and 2000. In absolute terms, relative abundance decreased from 1.48 to 1.28. In other words, an advanced birder who spent 2.5 hours birdwatching at 100 random locations throughout the region would have likely seen around 148 wood thrushes in 1970 and 128 in 2000. This result is quite puzzling. How can relative abundance have increased and the number of birds seen in our example decreased? The answer has to do with the nature of averages and the pattern of change in the relative abundance of the wood thrush. For example, if our birder started in Minneapolis, Minnesota, and spent 2.5 hours *randomly* roaming the roadsides, on average she would have seen slightly fewer birds in 2000 given the spatial arrangement of change in relative abundance. On the other hand, if our birder had driven due east she would have driven into prime habitat and would have seen more birds in 2000. This pattern also holds true in large portions of Wisconsin, Michigan, Missouri, and Illinois. Therefore, while this condition seems contradictory, it is, on average, altogether reasonable.

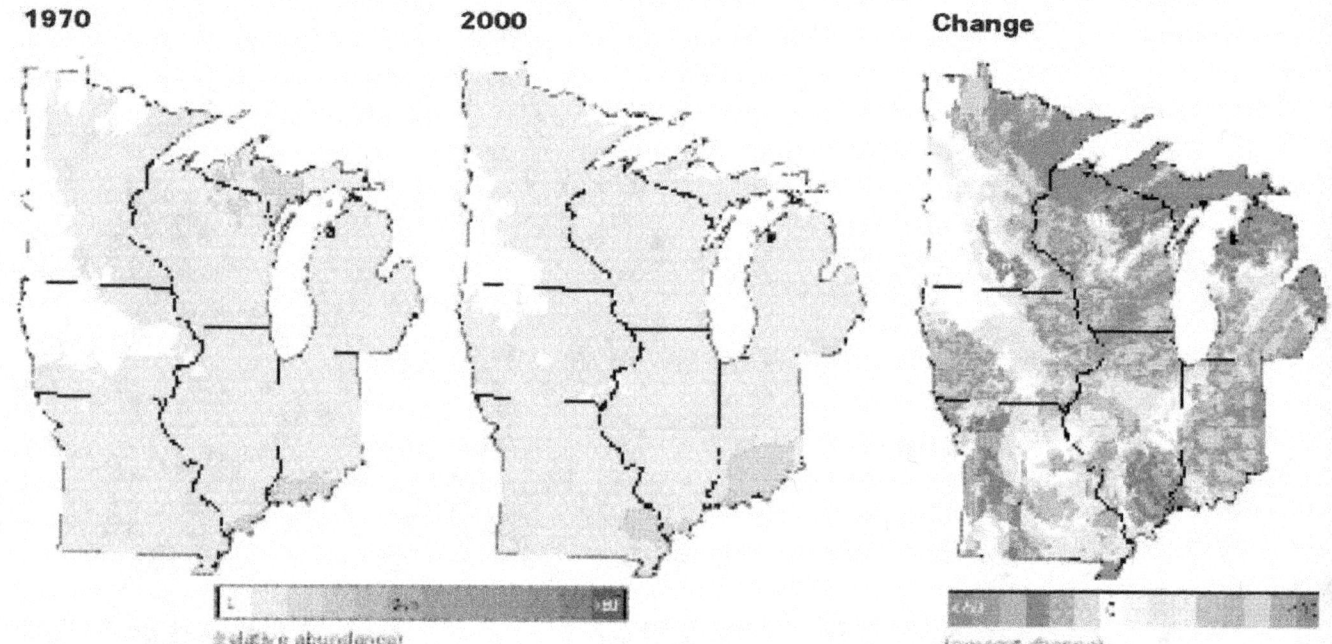

1970 **2000** **Change**

Figure 44. Estimated relative abundance of wood thrush, 1970 and 2000. Percent change in relative abundance, 1970-2000. Data source: USGS Breeding Bird Survey.

Introduction

The Changing Midwest Assessment is unique among natural resource assessments in that both bio-physical and social landscapes were monitored. Social landscapes, while seemingly more conceptual in nature than biophysical landscapes, are nonetheless very real. The social landscape is comprised of features that can be observed and measured directly, such as the number of people or houses on a tract of land, and others that are psychological in nature, such as how people perceive or value a tract of land.

The psychological dimension, of course, is the major difference between biophysical and social land-scapes. The psychological dimension is what makes social landscapes difficult to measure, but it also provides invaluable insights to natural resource managers and elected officials who struggle on a daily basis with the task of making decisions that are ecologically sustainable, economically viable, and socially acceptable to the greatest extent possible, which, at its foundation, is what Ecosystem Management is all about.

In monitoring the social landscape of the Midwest, we focused on demographic, economic, and social data. The key questions we addressed were:

- How has population density changed?

- How has housing density changed?

- How has seasonal housing density changed?

- How has the role of frontier industries changed?

- Is a conservation economy emerging?

- How have attitudes about the environment changed?

Demographic Trends

We evaluated tends in population, housing density, and seasonal housing density using county data from the U.S. Census Bureau from 1980 and 2000. This work was conducted in cooperation with Roger Hammer (Department of Rural Sociology) and Volker Radeloff (Department of Forest Ecology and Management) of the University of Wisconsin, School of Natural Resources (www.wisc.edu), and was supported by John Dwyer and Susan Stewart of the North Central Research Station (http://www.ncrs.fs.fed.us/4902/).

Economic Trends

To illustrate how the economy of the Midwest has changed, we examined what some have referred to as the frontier economy and the conservation economy. In particular, we calculated change in personal income derived from forestry and lumber and wood products (frontier economy) and amusement and recreation (conservation economy), which are classes of jobs within the manufacturing and service sectors, respectively, as defined by the U.S. Department of Commerce. County-level economic data were retrieved from the Bureau of Economic Analysis (www.bea.doc.gov) and the Bureau of Labor Statistics (www.bls.gov).

Social Trends

Although there are many types of landscape change, we were particularly interested in understanding how people feel about urban sprawl. According to the Pew Center for Civic Journalism (www.pewcenter.org), urban sprawl is among the most frequently cited local problems in the country. However, little work has been done to document what it is about urban sprawl that people are concerned about. In order to identify the specific concerns that people have about urban sprawl, and to monitor how those concerns have changed over time, we conducted a computer guided content analysis using InfoTrend Software and the Lexis-Nexis online database. We identified the most common concerns about urban sprawl between 1995 and 2001.

How Has Population Density Changed?

People are the essence of social landscapes and the dominant force that shapes biophysical landscapes; therefore, it is essential that we understand how the population and population density of the Midwest are changing. To be clear, population data describe *how many people* live in the region, whereas population density data provide insights into *where* people live.

Population Density: 1980

Approximately 42.8 million people lived in the region in 1980. At the county level, population density ranged from just over 2 people per square mile to more than 6,800 people per square mile (figure 45, 1980). Most of the counties in the region–about 60 percent–had a population density of fewer than 50 people per square mile, which is equivalent to an average of 1 person per 12.8 acres.

Population Density: 2000

About 47.2 million people lived in the region in 2000. Population density ranged from 2.5 people per square mile to more than 5,600 people per square mile (figure 45, 2000). Approximately 55 percent of the counties in the region had a population density of fewer than 50 people per square mile.

At the county level, change in population density ranged from a loss of almost 1,000 people per square mile–in metro areas such as Detroit and St. Louis–to an increase of more than 700 people per square mile in the sprawling suburbs of Detroit, St. Louis, Milwaukee, Indianapolis, Minneapolis-St. Paul, and Chicago.

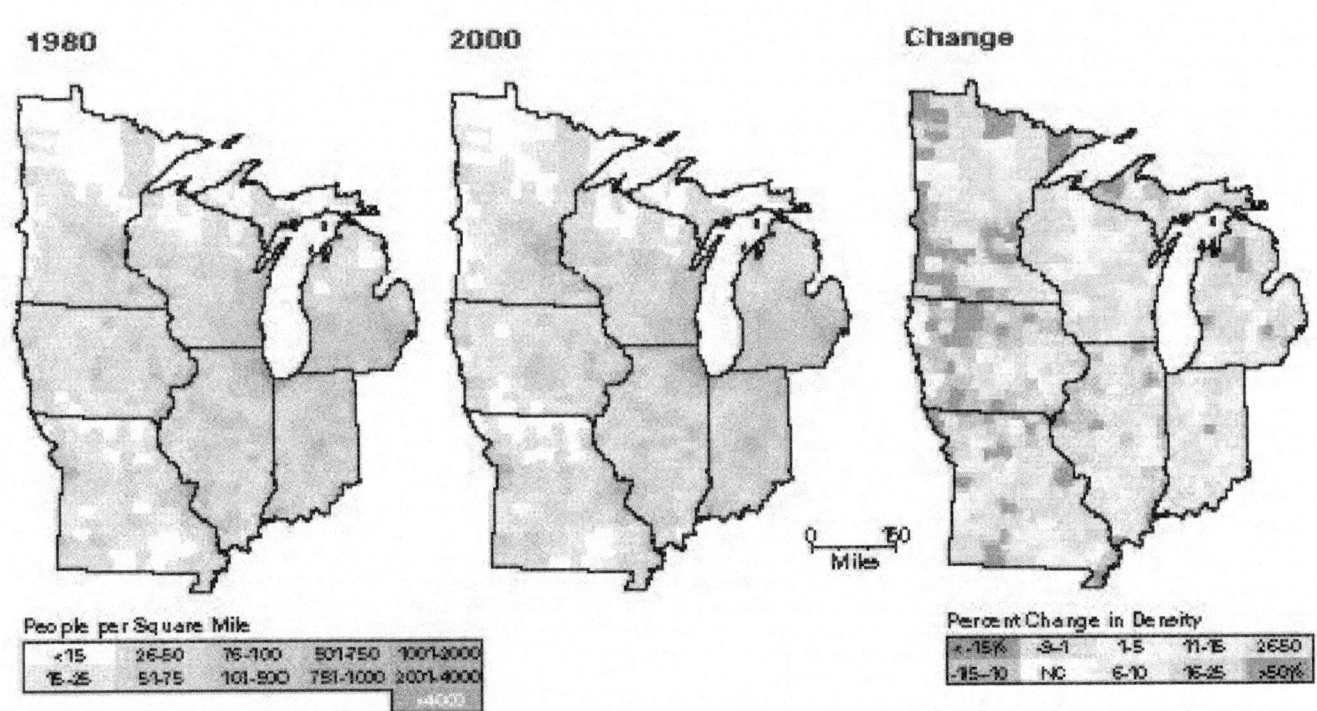

1980 **2000** **Change**

People per Square Mile

<15	26-50	76-100	501-750	1001-2000
16-25	51-75	101-500	751-1000	2001-4000
				>4000

Percent Change in Density

<-15%	-3-1	1-5	11-15	26-50
-15-10	NC	6-10	16-25	>50%

Figure 45. Population density, 1980 and 2000. Percent change in population density, 1980-2000. Data source: U.S. Census Bureau.

Change in Population Density

Overall, the population of the region increased by slightly more than 10 percent between 1980 and 2000. At the county level, change in population density ranged from a decrease of 25 percent to an increase of 142 percent (figure 45, Change). To put this into perspective, consider that absolute change in population density ranged from a loss of almost 1,600 people per square mile in metro areas such as Detroit and St. Louis to an increase of more than 700 people per square mile in the sprawling suburbs of Detroit, St. Louis, Milwaukee, Indianapolis, Minneapolis-St. Paul, and Chicago.

Further, it is interesting to note that while the majority of counties experienced moderate levels of change that was spatially nondescript, change in the "hotspots" occurred in two distinct spatial patterns. A sprawling pattern is evident in Indianapolis, Chicago, and Minneapolis-St. Paul, whereas a pattern of urban flight is evident in Milwaukee, Detroit, and St. Louis. For example, Hennepin County, which contains the urban core of Minneapolis, experienced moderate levels of growth, and counties on the suburban fringe grew rapidly (figure 46A); conversely, the urban core in St. Louis experienced dramatic declines in population density and counties on the urban fringe grew rapidly (figure 46B).

Interpreting Change in Population Density

At the State level, change in population density ranged from an increase of less than 1 percent in Iowa to an increase of almost 21 percent in Minnesota (figure 47). To put this into perspective, consider that annual change in population density ranged from an increase of less than 1 person per square mile in Iowa to more than 17 in Illinois (figure 48).

Figure 46. Spatial patterns of change in population density, 1980-2000. Maps portray urban sprawl (A) in Minneapolis, Minnesota, and urban flight (B) in St. Louis, Missouri. Data source: U.S. Census Bureau.

A. Urban Sprawl

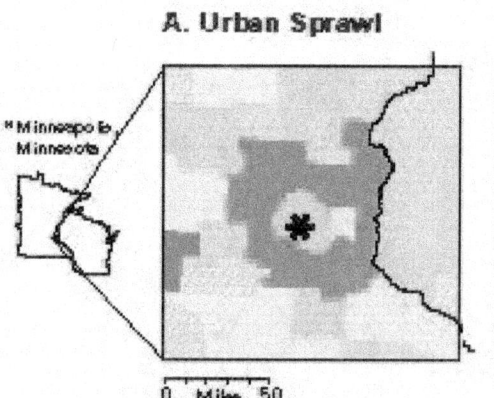

B. Urban Flight

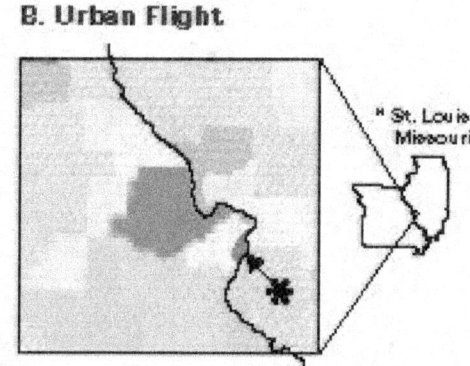

0   Miles   50

Percent Change in Population Density

<-15%	-9-1	1-5	11-15	25-50
-15--10	NC	6-10	16-25	>50%

Percent Change

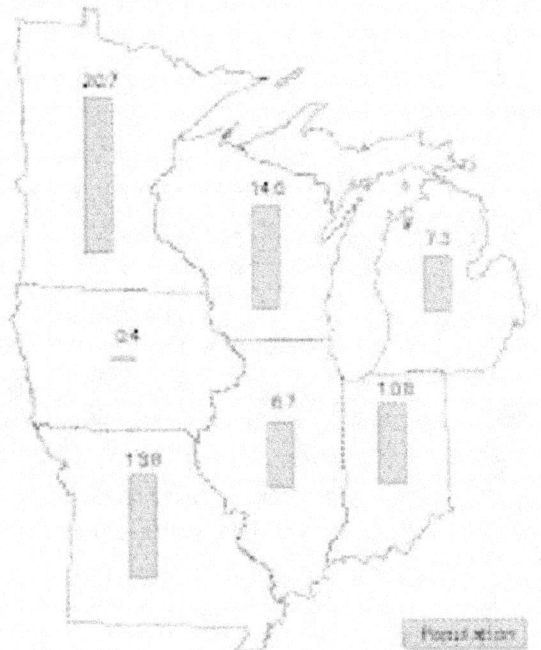

Figure 47. Percent change in population density, 1980-2000. Data source: U.S. Census Bureau.

Change
(people/square mile)

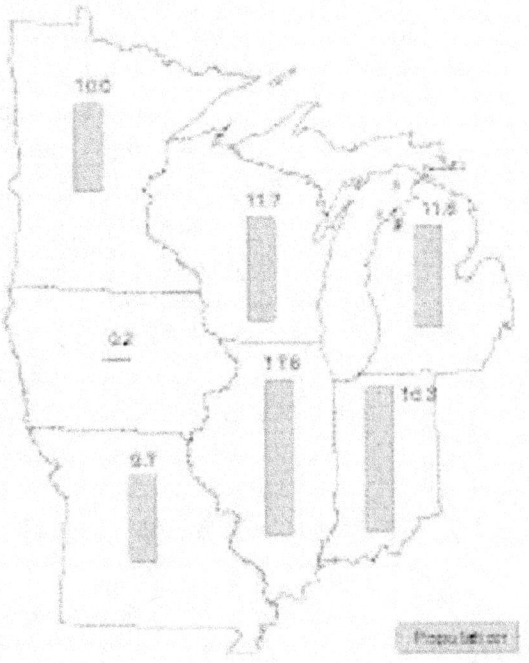

Figure 48. Annual change in population density, 1980-2000. Data source: U.S. Census Bureau.

How Has Housing Density Changed?

Although people are undoubtedly the essence of social landscapes, there is a long-standing philosophical debate in social science circles as to whether or not people are a natural part of the landscape. Those who argue that people are "unnatural" point to the fact that we leave a disproportionately large footprint on the biophysical landscape. And, whichever camp you are in, there is little doubt that the homes we build do have tremendous visual and ecological impact on the biophysical landscape. The design and location of our homes also reflect what we value as individuals and as a society. For these reasons it is important to understand how housing and housing density have changed over time. The U.S. Census Bureau defines a housing unit as a house, apartment, group of rooms, or single room that is occupied or intended for occupancy as separate living quarters.

To grasp the significance of county-level housing densities in excess of 110 units per square mile, consider that in Cook County, if each housing unit was a traditional single family structure, the *entire* biophysical landscape would be subdivided into one-third acre lots.

Total Housing Density: 1980

There were approximately 16.2 million housing units in the region in 1980. At the county level, housing density ranged from just over 1 unit per square mile to more than 3,050 units per square mile (figure 49, 1980). A majority of counties in the region had housing densities between 5 and 15 units per square mile, which corresponds to an average of 1 unit every 64 acres. Approximately 5 percent of all counties had a housing density of less than 5 units per square mile, which is equivalent to an average of 1 housing unit per 582 acres. For example, the housing density in Lake of the Woods County, Minnesota, was 1.1 units per square mile. On the other end of the spectrum, just over 7 percent of all counties had a housing density greater than 110 units per square mile. To put this into perspective, consider Cook County, Illinois, which had an average housing density of 2,083 units per square mile. To grasp the significance of county-level housing densities in excess of 110 units per square mile, consider that in Cook County, if each housing unit was a traditional single family structure, the *entire* biophysical landscape would be subdivided into one-third acre lots.

Total Housing Density: 2000

In 2000, there were over 19.7 million housing units in the region. At the county level, housing density ranged from just under 2 units per square mile to more than 2,650 units per square mile (figure 49, 2000). The majority of counties in the region had a housing density between 5 and 15 units per square mile, while approximately 4.5 percent had housing densities of less than 5 units per square mile, and almost 9.5 percent had housing densities of 110 or more units per square mile.

Change in Total Housing Density

Housing density increased in each of the seven States in the region, by an average of nearly 22 percent region wide. At the county level, change in total housing density ranged from a decrease of 15 percent to an increase of just over 150 percent (figure 49, Change). More than 80 percent of counties in the region experienced an increase in housing density; however, large-scale increases in excess of 100 percent were most prevalent in the Lakes District of Wisconsin, north of the Twin Cities in Minnesota, and the northern one-third of the Lower Peninsula of Michigan. For example, consider Forest County, Wisconsin, where the number of housing units increased by 116 percent, from fewer than 4,000 housing

units in 1980 to more than 8,300 in 2000. Losses in housing density were concentrated along western Minnesota (the eastern edge of the wheat belt), throughout Iowa, northern Missouri, and western Illinois.

To put this into perspective, consider that the change in the total number of housing units in Michigan alone would have required the conversion of approximately 392,000 acres of land, assuming each new housing unit had an average lot size of 0.5 acres and occupied a previously undeveloped site.

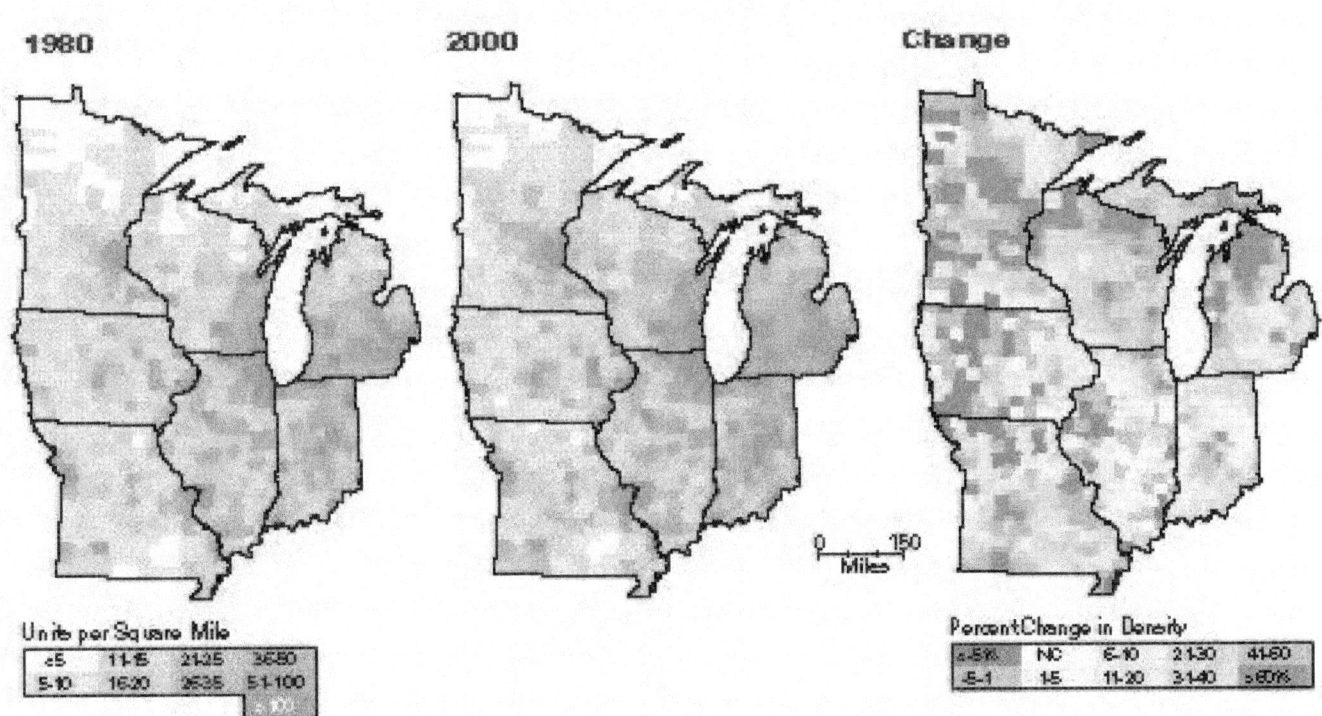

1980

2000

Change

Units per Square Mile

<5	11-15	21-35	36-50
5-10	16-20	26-35	51-100
			>100

Percent Change in Density

<-5%	NC	6-10	21-30	41-60
-5-1	1-5	11-20	31-40	>60%

Figure 49. Housing density 1980 and 2000. Percent change in housing density, 1980-2000. Data source: U.S. Census Bureau.

Interpreting Change in Housing Density

At the State level, change in housing density ranged from an increase of nearly 10 percent in Iowa to an increase of 35 percent in Minnesota (figure 50). In absolute terms, change in the total number of housing units ranged from an increase of 111,200 units in Iowa to 783,600 units in Michigan. To put this into perspective, consider that the change in the total number of housing units in Michigan alone would have required the conversion of approximately 392,000 acres of land, assuming each new housing unit had an average lot size of 0.5 acres and occupied a previously undeveloped site (figure 51).

Percent Change

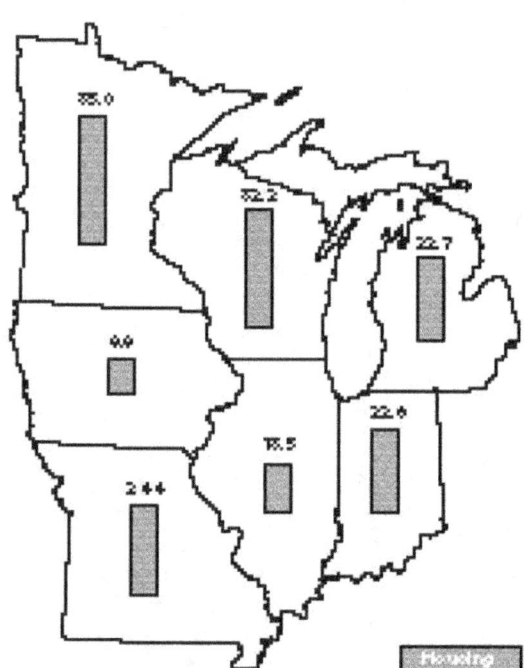

Figure 50. Percent change in housing density, 1980-2000. Data source: U.S. Census Bureau.

Change
(acres)

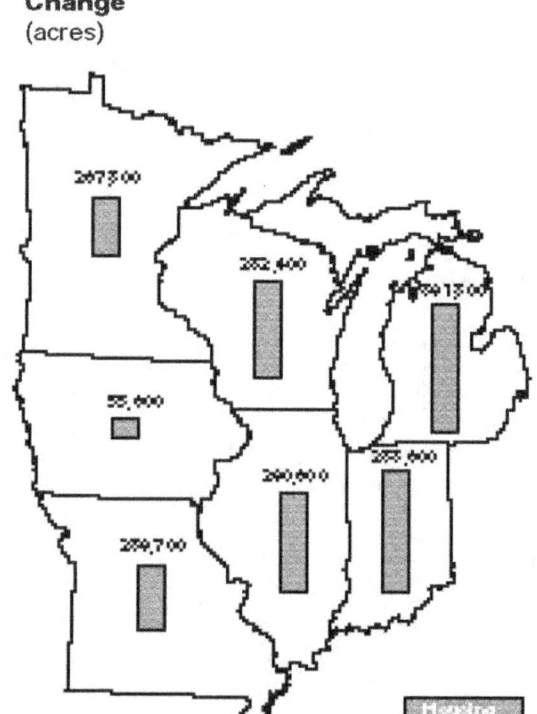

Figure 51. Estimated area of land converted (acres) to urban based on change in total number of new housing units, 1980-2000. Data source: U.S. Census Bureau.

How Has Seasonal Housing Density Changed?

Historically, home ownership was the crux of the American Dream. Today the dream seems to have expanded to include a seasonal home with a lake view. And of all the special places in the Midwest where one would dream of building a seasonal home, perhaps the one most often spoken of is the magical place we call "The Northwoods" or more simply "Up North." Each year anglers, hunters, and outdoor enthusiasts of all kinds from within the region and across the Nation spend millions of visitor days Up North. While many of these visitors stay in hotels or other temporary quarters, seasonal housing units are becoming more and more common. The U.S. Census Bureau defines seasonal housing units as living quarters that are held for weekend or other occasional use throughout the year; second homes may or may not be classified as seasonal housing units.

Seasonal Housing Density: 1980

There were more than 192,000 seasonal housing units in the region in 1980. At the county level, the density of seasonal housing units ranged from less than 1 unit per square mile to more than 18 units per square mile (figure 52, 1980). The vast majority of counties–nearly 90 percent–had a seasonal housing density of less than 1 unit per square mile. Of the counties with a seasonal housing density greater than 1 unit per square mile, 75 percent were in northern Minnesota, Wisconsin, and Michigan.

Seasonal Housing Density: 2000

In 2000, the number of seasonal housing units in the region increased to nearly 628,000. At the county level, the density of seasonal housing units ranged from less than 1 unit per square mile to more than 21 units per square mile (figure 52, 2000). The majority of counties–69 percent–had a seasonal housing density of less than

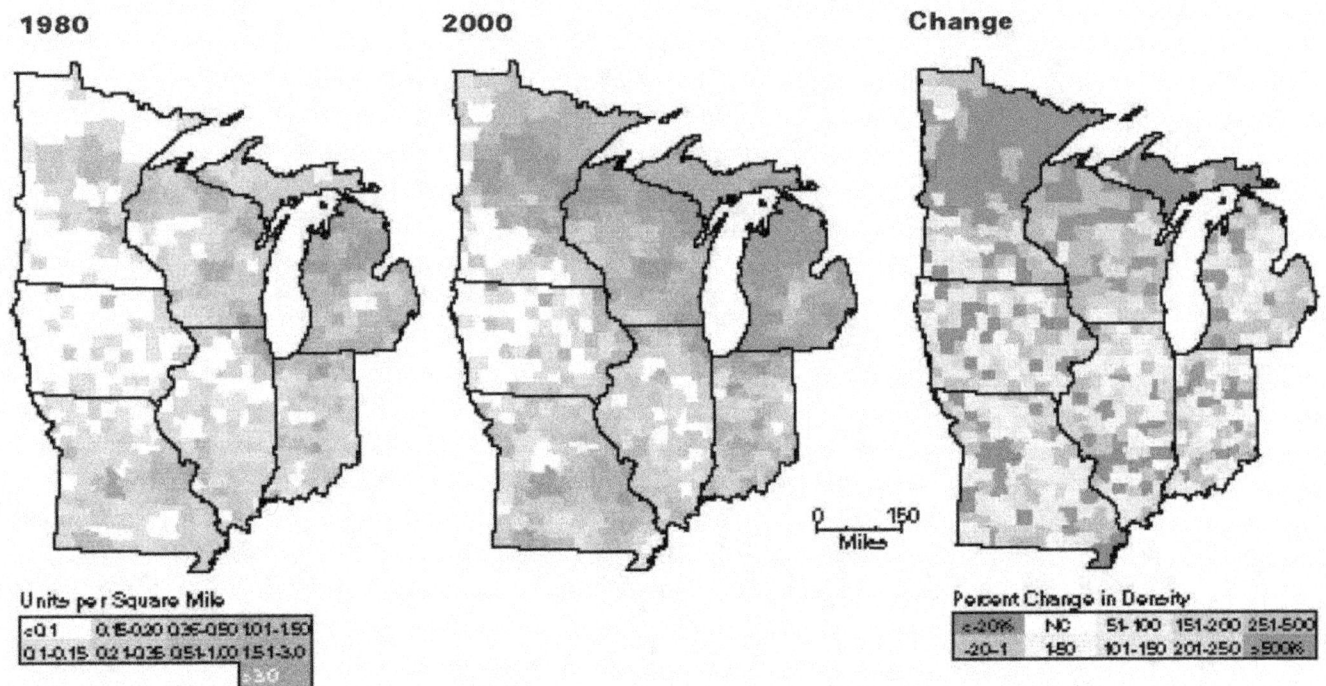

Figure 52. Density of seasonal housing units, 1980 and 2000. Percent change in density of seasonal housing units. Data source: U.S. Census Bureau.

Addendum

Changing Midwest Assessment, GTR-NC-250

Seasonal Housing Density

The maps depicting change in the density of seasonal housing units must be interpreted with care. The definition of a seasonal housing unit used by the Census Bureau changed significantly in 1990. Furthermore, the tabular data published by the Census Bureau and the definitions provided with those data exhibit inconsistencies such that it is very difficult to know exactly how the data for seasonal housing in the 1980 census should be compared to the data in the 1990 and 2000 censuses. Because of the incongruities between the definitions in 1980 and 2000, the magnitude of the changes shown in the change map on page 57 of the Changing Midwest Assessment (figure 52) likely exceeds the actual change. However, we believe that the relative rates of change are valid and demonstrate the variations in relative rates of change across the Midwest. For example, we are confident that counties shown as having >500

percent change in the density of seasonal housing (red counties) did experience the greatest growth in seasonal housing density, though the magnitude of the change was likely much less than 500 percent.

Figure 52a (below) shows the change in seasonal housing density between 1990 and 2000. The change map looks markedly different than that shown in figure 52 (page 57) for several reasons. First, the same definition of seasonal housing units is used in 1990 and in 2000, reducing the likelihood that the same housing unit receiving the same use would be classified as seasonal in one census and permanent in the next. Changes in social trends also give rise to differences; seasonal housing density approached a saturation point in the upper Midwest in the 1980s, resulting in much slower growth during the 1990s. Furthermore, many housing units that were seasonal homes in 1990 had become permanent homes by 2000, a trend that is reflected in the declines in seasonal housing density seen in many counties that had high seasonal housing densities in 1990.

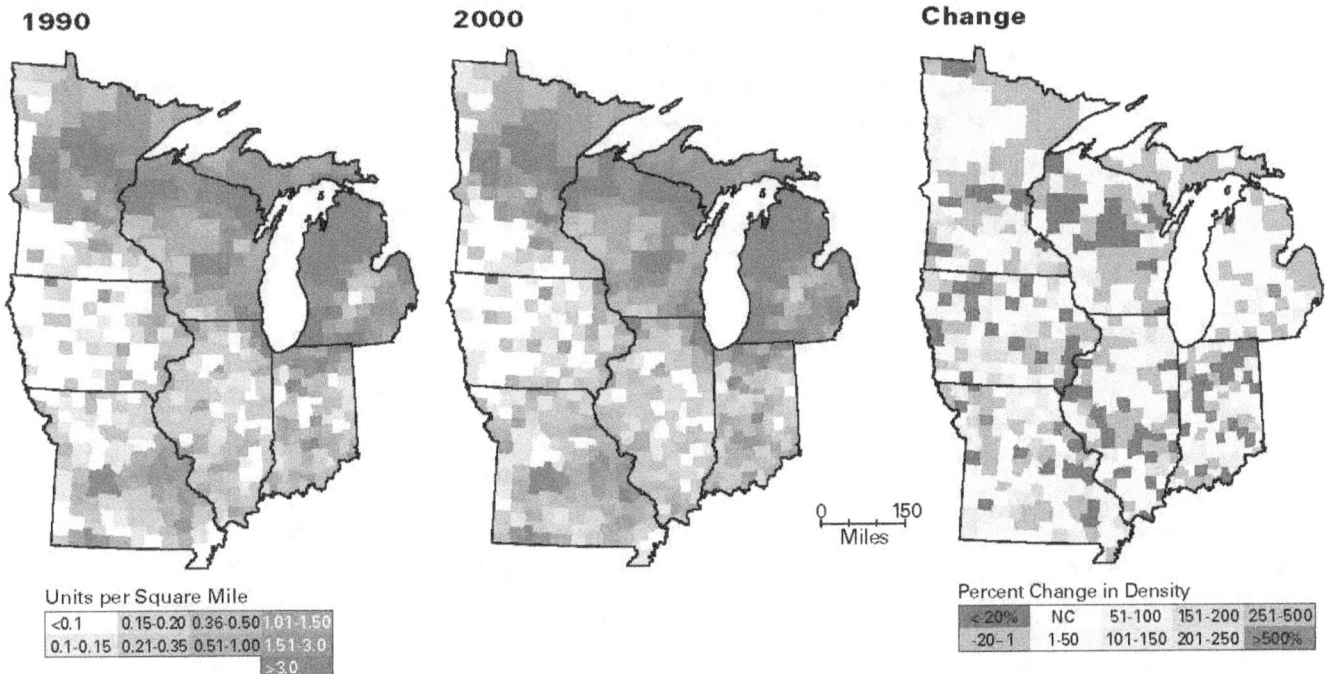

Figure 52a. Density of seasonal housing units, 1990 and 2000. Percent change in density of seasonal housing units. Data source: U.S. Census Bureau.

1 unit per square mile. Of the counties with a seasonal housing density greater than 1 unit per square mile, nearly 72 percent were in Minnesota, Wisconsin, and Michigan.

In Minnesota alone the number of seasonal housing units increased by more than 90,000. To grasp the significance of a change of this magnitude, consider that these new units would have required the conversion of approximately 45,000 acres of land, assuming that each new unit had a lot size of 0.5 acres and occupied a previously undeveloped site.

Change in Seasonal Housing Density

At the county level, percent change in the density of seasonal housing units ranged from a decrease of 69 percent to an increase of more than 2,500 percent (figure 52, Change). More than 82 percent of the counties in the region experienced an increase in the density of seasonal housing units. Of the counties that experienced increases in the density of seasonal housing units, nearly 20 percent had increases that exceeded 500 percent; the majority of these counties were in northern Minnesota, northern Wisconsin, and the Upper Peninsula of Michigan.

Interpreting Change in Seasonal Housing Density

Overall, the number of seasonal housing units increased by more than 435,000 between 1980 and 2000. Region wide, the density of seasonal housing units increased by 225 percent.

At the State level, change in the density of seasonal housing units ranged from approximately 50 percent in Illinois to more than 600 percent in Minnesota (figure 53). To put this into perspective, consider that in Minnesota alone the number of seasonal housing units increased by more than 90,000. To grasp the significance of a change of this magnitude, consider that these new units would have required the conversion of approximately 45,000 acres of land, assuming that each new unit had a lot size of 0.5 acres and occupied a previously undeveloped site (figure 54).

Percent Change

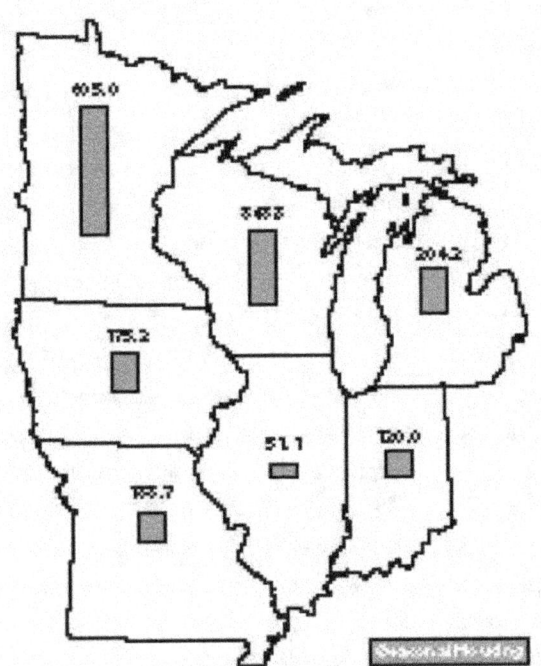

Figure 53. Percent change in density of seasonal housing units, 1980-2000. Data source: U.S. Census Bureau.

Change
(acres)

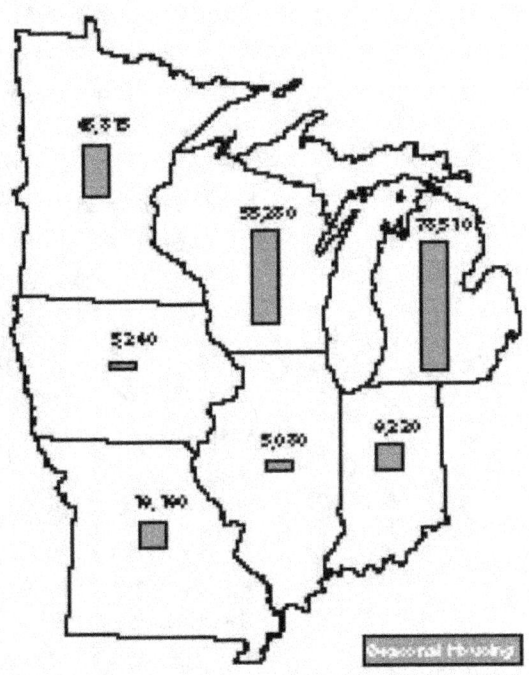

Figure 54. Estimated area of land converted (acres) to urban based on change in the number of seasonal housing units, 1980-2000. Data source: U.S. Census Bureau.

How Have Frontier Industries Changed?

Overall, the biophysical landscape of the Midwest is dominated by agriculture, but the Lakes States, and to a lesser degree southern Missouri and Indiana, are heavily forested. In fact, over half of the landscape in Michigan is classified as forestland (figure 7) and the area of forest is increasing across the region (figure 20). Accordingly, the forestry and lumber and wood products industries, hereafter referred to as frontier industries, have always been important components of the culture and economy of the Midwest. This is especially true in timber-dependent communities of the northwoods (figure 55), but the frontier economy is growing throughout the Midwest. For example, consider that there are currently over 6,000 business establishments in the Midwest that specialize in forestry and lumber and wood products, including more than 2,000 mills. These facilities directly employ more than 144,000 people, and process approximately 8 percent of the wood products that are consumed in America (Shifley and Sullivan 2002). Further, consider that between 1980 and 2000 frontier industries grew faster than the total industrial average for the Midwest in terms of number of employees and total wages earned (table 3).

Frontier Industries: 1980

Total personal income in the region exceeded $439 billion in 1980. Approximately $1.5 billion (0.34 percent) was attributable to frontier industries, the vast majority of which was attributable to the lumber and wood products industry. At the county level, per capita income derived from lumber and wood products ranged from less than $2 to more than $887 (figure 56, 1980). Per capita income from forestry ranged from less than $1 to just under $29 (figure 57, 1980). At the State level, the average annual income of individuals employed in the lumber and wood products industry ranged from $10,479 in Missouri to $16,734 in Minnesota; average annual income in forestry ranged from $13,421 in Missouri to $18,364 in Wisconsin.

Frontier Industries: 2000

In 2000, total personal income in the region exceeded $1.4 trillion. Approximately $5.2 billion (0.36 percent) was attributable to frontier industries. Once again, earnings from lumber and wood products far exceeded earnings from forestry. At the county level, per capita income derived from lumber and wood products ranged from $4 to more than $3,300 (figure 56, 2000).

Figure 55. Map depicts percent of total personal income derived from frontier industries in northern Wisconsin. Data source: U.S. Bureau of Economic Analysis.

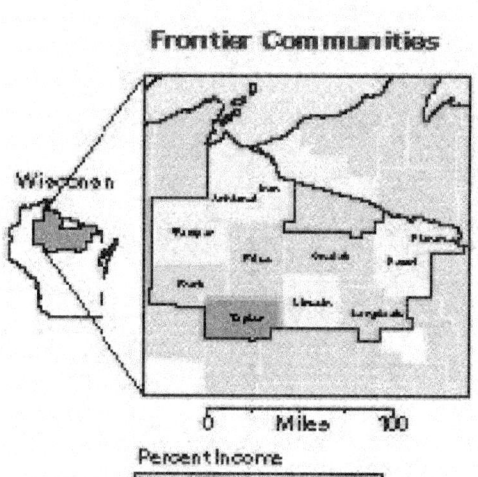

Frontier Communities

Wisconsin

0   Miles   100

Percent Income
None <5% 5-10 11-15 ≥ 15%

Table 3. Comparison of changes (%) in frontier industries and the average for all industries in the Midwest, 1980-2000. Data source: U.S. Bureau of Economic Analysis.

Percent Change 1980-2000		
	Frontier industries	All industries
Number of Establishments	47	56
Number of Employees	73	35
Total Wages	294	208
Average Annual Income	119	126

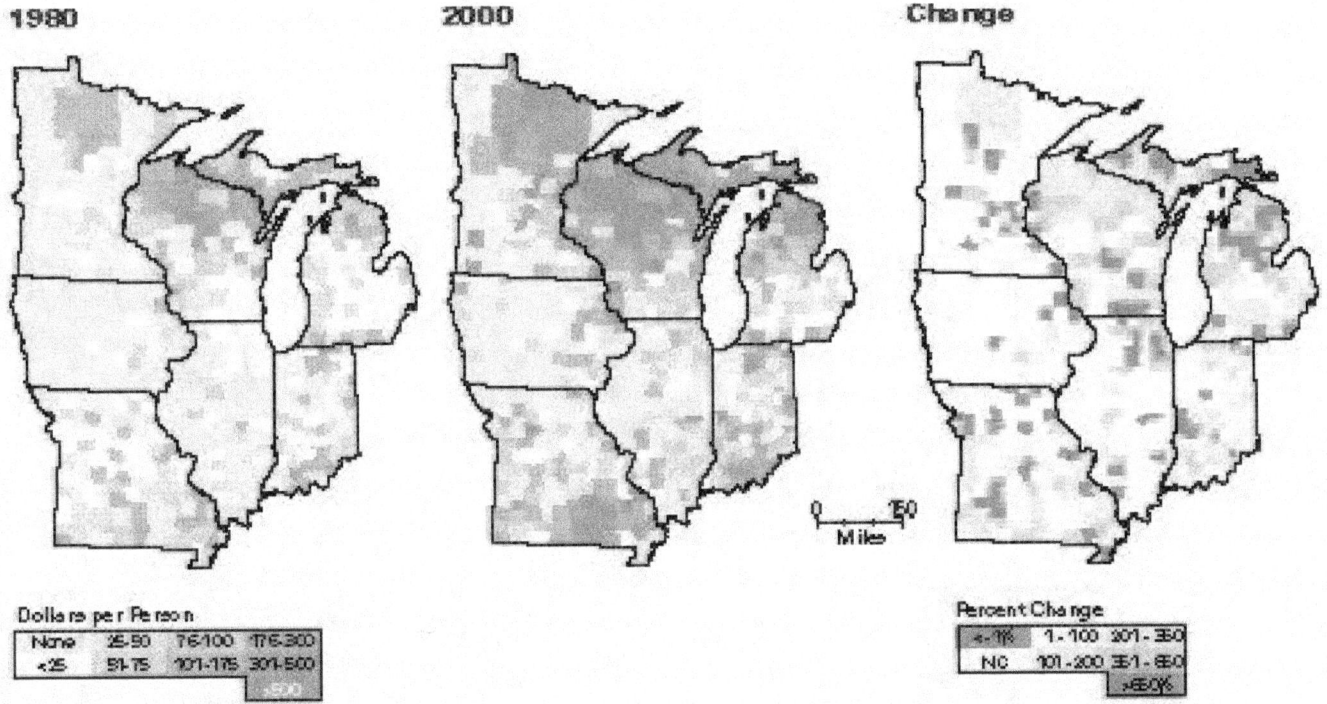

Figure 56. Per capita income from lumber and wood products, 1980 and 2000. Percent change in per capita income, 1980-2000. Data source: U.S. Bureau of Economic Analysis.

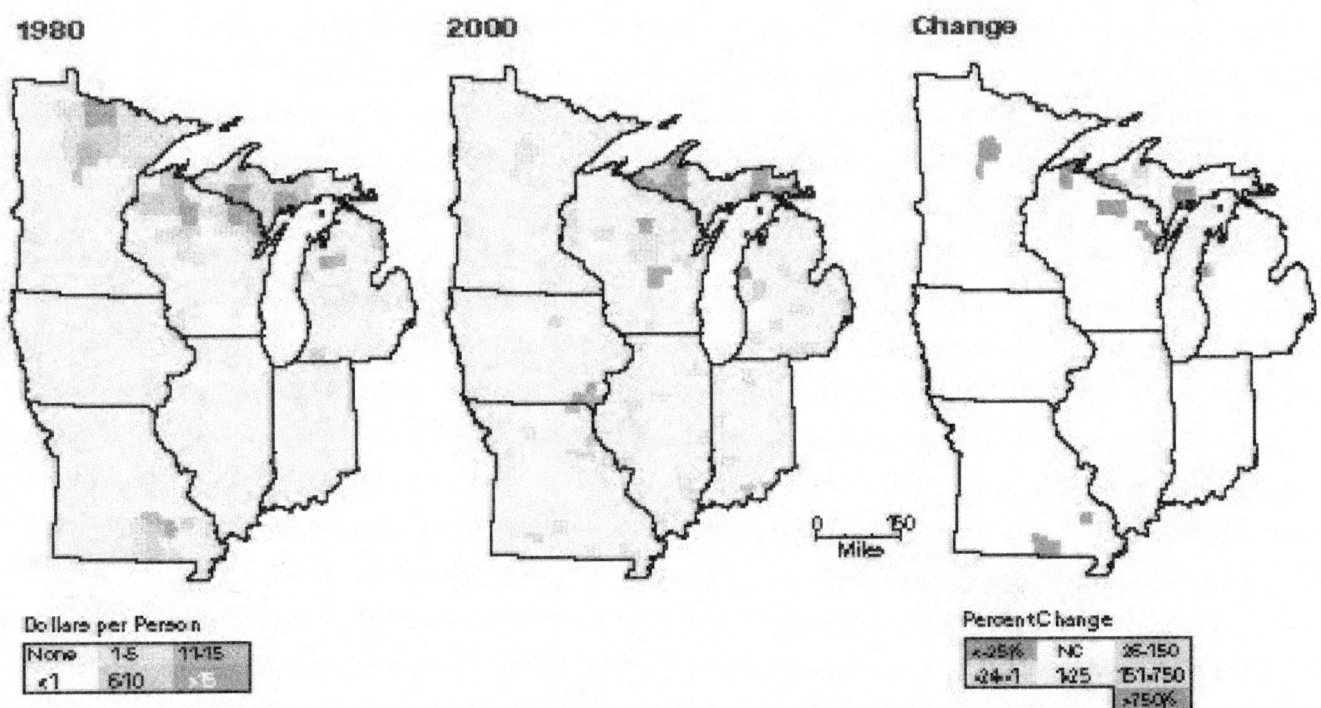

Figure 57. Per capita income from forestry, 1980 and 2000. Percent change in per capita income, 1980-2000. Data source: U.S. Bureau of Economic Analysis.

Per capita income from forestry ranged from less than $1 to more than $150 (figure 57, 2000). At the State level, the average annual income of individuals employed in the lumber and wood products industry ranged from $22,736 in Missouri to $35,896 in Minnesota; average annual income in forestry ranged from $13,792 in Indiana to $24,083 in Missouri.

Change in the Frontier Economy

At the county level, percent change in per capita income derived from lumber and wood products ranged from a decrease of 100 percent to an increase of more than 24,000 percent (figure 56, Change). To put this into perspective, consider Douglas County, Illinois, where personal income from lumber and wood products increased from $61,000 in 1980 to nearly $15,000,000 in 2000.

Percent change in per capita income derived from forestry ranged from a decrease of 100 percent to an increase of more than 2,100 percent (figure 57, Change). To put this into perspective, consider Gogebic County, Michigan, where personal income from forestry increased from $52,000 in 1980 to nearly $1,036,000 in 2000.

Percent Change

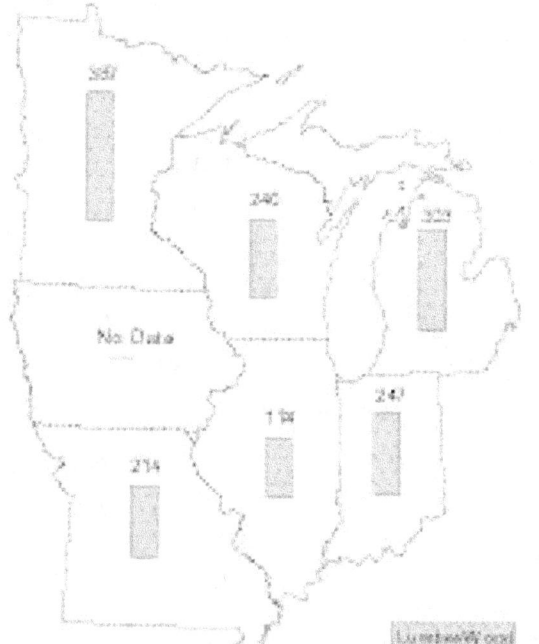

Figure 58. Percent change in personal income from lumber and wood products, 1980-2000. Data source: U.S. Bureau of Economic Analysis.

Change (million dollars)

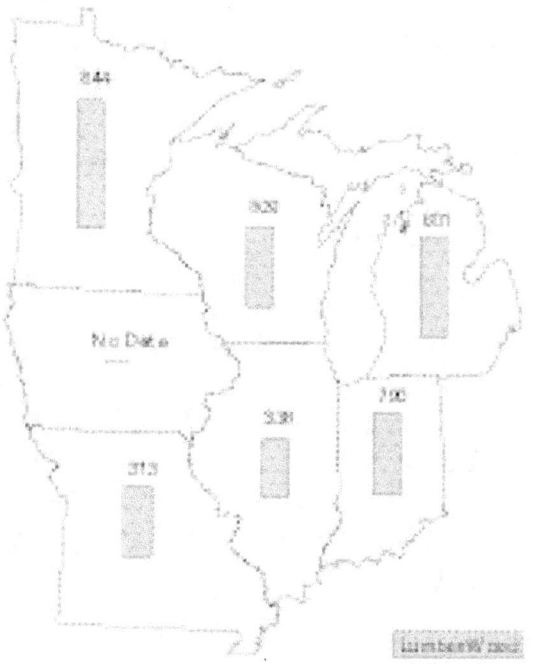

Figure 59. Change in personal income from lumber and wood products, 1980-2000. Data source: U.S. Bureau of Economic Analysis.

Interpreting Change in the Frontier Economy

To put these changes into perspective, consider that total personal income increased by 219 percent region wide between 1980 and 2000. Personal income associated with the frontier economy increased by 241 percent.

At the State level, percent change in personal income associated with lumber and wood products ranged from an increase of 174 percent in Illinois to an increase of 387 percent in Minnesota (figure 58, page 62). In absolute terms, the largest increase occurred in Minnesota, where personal income increased by nearly $844 million, from $217 million in 1980 to nearly $1.1 billion in 2000 (figure 59, page 62).

Percent change in personal income associated with forestry ranged from an increase of 56 percent in Missouri to an increase of 491 percent in Indiana (figure 60). In absolute terms, the largest increase occurred in Michigan, where personal income derived from forestry increased by nearly $16 million, from $6.2 million in 1980 to more than $22 million in 2000 (figure 61).

Percent Change

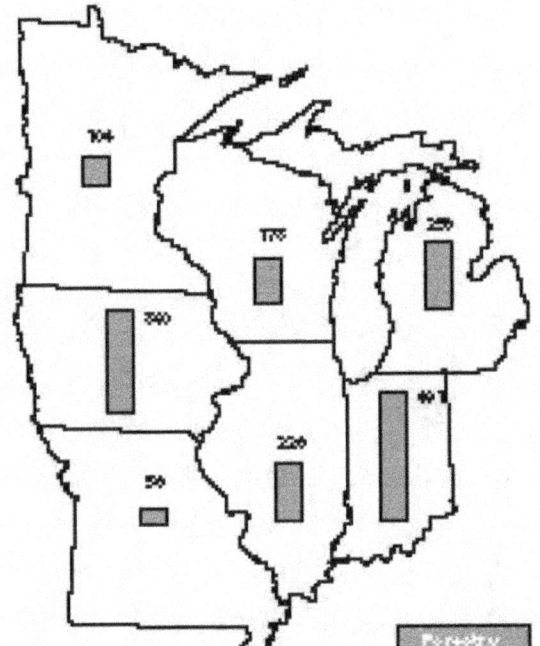

Figure 60. Percent change in personal income from forestry, 1980-2000. Data source: U.S. Bureau of Economic Analysis.

Change
(million dollars)

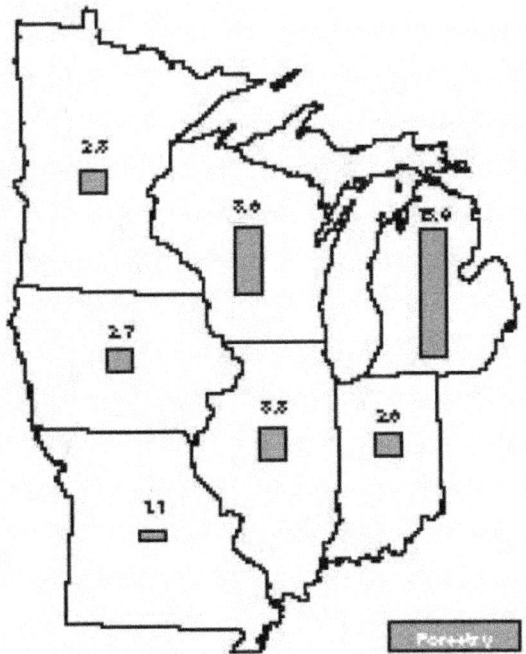

Figure 61. Change in personal income from forestry, 1980-2000. Data source: U.S. Bureau of Economic Analysis.

Is a Conservation Economy Emerging?

Historically, the economy of the Midwest has been frontier oriented, based largely on agriculture, axes, and automobiles. If there is any doubt about the frontier mentality of midwesterners, consider that the region is equally well known as the breadbasket, the home of Paul Bunyan, and the automobile capital of the world. The region remains frontier oriented to some extent, and it will remain so as long as homes are built with wood, farmers continue to farm, and automakers produce automobiles. However, attitudes about resource extraction and development have clearly changed over the past 40 years, and there is little doubt that the economy has diversified. In particular, as attitudes about the environment have changed, and as levels of disposable income have increased, a conservation-based economy has emerged in the Midwest.

A conservation-based economy is service oriented, including tourism, amusement, and recreation services, rather than manufacturing oriented. And just as the Midwest is well suited for the frontier economy, it is well suited for a conservation-based economy. In addition to the abundance of forested land and water, the region also has a highly developed recreational infrastructure that includes 30 National Park Service destinations, 10 National Forests and Grasslands, more than 500 State Parks, thousands of scientific and natural areas, nature preserves, archeological sites, wildlife preserves, and one of the largest State Forest systems in the country. Collectively, there are over 50,000 campsites, 26,000 lakes and reservoirs of at least 10 acres, and 5,000 miles of trails. Not surprisingly, millions of hunters, anglers, and outdoor enthusiasts from within the region and across

Economic Impact 2000
(billion dollars)

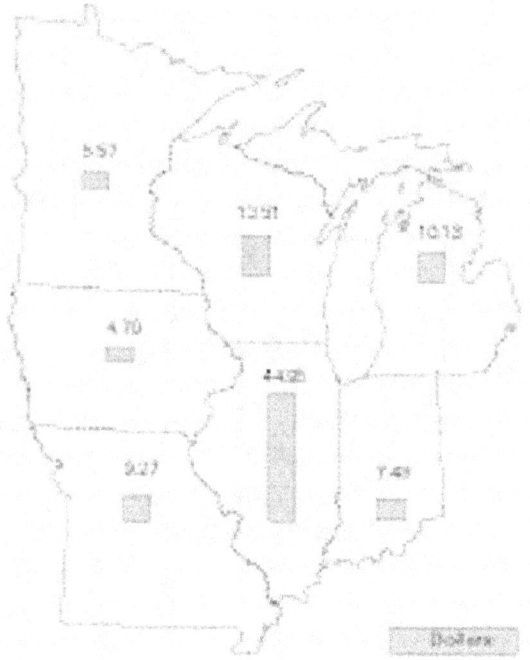

Figure 62. Total economic impact of tourism (billion dollars), 2000.

Visitor Days 2000
(million days)

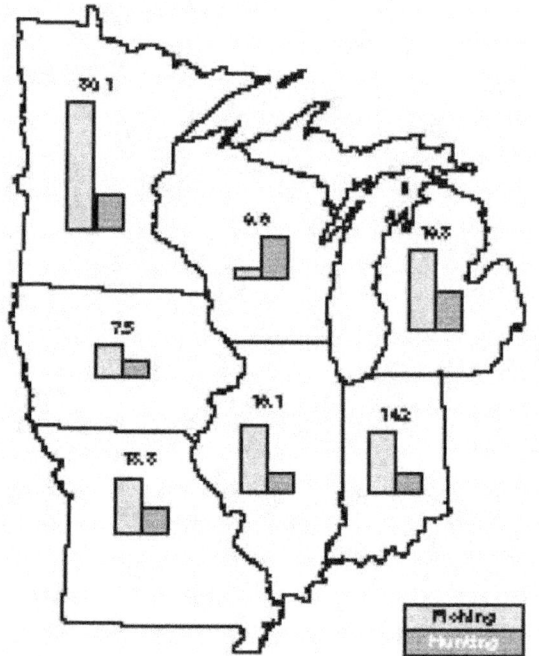

Figure 63. Number of fishing and hunting visitor days (million days), 2000.

the Nation spend hundreds of millions of visitor days, and billions of dollars, recreating in the Midwest each year (figures 62 and 63).

Recreation-Dependent Communities
In addition to the massive infrastructure of public parks, forests, and recreation areas, there are over 3,100 establishments that specialize in amusement and recreation, as defined by the Bureau of Labor Statistics, employing 31,000 people. Additionally, there are thousands of souvenir shops and eating and drinking establishments that are dependent on tourists and recreationists that are not classified as amusement and recreation establishments by the Bureau of Labor Statistics; these establishments create an estimated 1 million seasonal and permanent jobs. Given all this, it is not surprising that the Midwest has one of the highest concentrations of recreation-dependent communities in the country, or that the number of such communities is on the rise (Johnson and Beale 2002). Recreation-dependent communities are characterized by high levels of personal income from

entertainment, recreation, lodging, eating and drinking establishments, and a high proportion of seasonal housing units (figure 64).

To identify the changing role and impact of conservation-based industries on the economy of the Midwest, we evaluated and mapped changes in the amount of personal income derived from amusement and recreation industries. For a detailed description of amusement and recreation industries, please visit the Bureau of Labor Statistics at www.bls.gov.

The region remains frontier oriented to some extent...however, attitudes about resource extraction and development have clearly changed over the past 40 years, and there is little doubt that the economy has diversified. In particular, as attitudes about the environment have changed, and as levels of disposable income have increased, a conservation-based economy has emerged.

Recreation-dependent Communities

 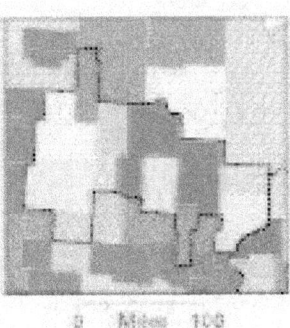

Minnesota

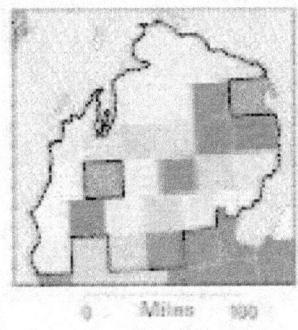 

Michigan

0   Miles   100

0   Miles   100

Percent Seasonal Housing

Figure 64. Examples of recreation-dependent communities in Minnesota and Michigan. Maps depict proportion of total housing units that are classified as seasonal. Adapted from Johnson and Beale (2002). Data source U.S. Census Bureau.

Amusement and Recreation Income: 1980

Total personal income in the region exceeded $439 billion in 1980. Approximately $1.4 billion (less than 0.5 percent) was attributable to the amusement and recreation industry. At the county level, per capita personal income derived from amusement and recreation ranged from less than $5.00 to more than $150 (figure 65, 1980). At the State level, the average annual income of individuals employed in the amusement and recreation industry ranged from $4,870 in Iowa to $8,225 in Missouri.

Amusement and Recreation Income: 2000

In 2000, total personal income in the region exceeded $1.4 trillion. Approximately $9.4 billion (0.67 percent) was attributable to the amusement and recreation industry. At the county level, per capita personal income derived from amusement and recreation ranged from less than $6.00 to more than $1,450.00 (figure 65, 2000). At the State level, the average annual income of individuals employed in amusement and recreation ranged from $11,291 in Iowa to $23,802 in Indiana.

Change in the Conservation Economy

Percent change in per capita personal income from amusement and recreation ranged from a decrease of 100 percent to an increase of more than 4,500 percent (figure 65, Change). To put this into perspective, consider Pine County, Minnesota, where personal income from amusement and recreation increased from $414,000 in 1980 to $44,100,000 in 2000.

Interpreting Change in the Conservation Economy

At the State level, percent change in personal income associated with amusement and recreation ranged from an increase of 460 percent in Illinois to an increase of more than 900 percent in Indiana (figure 66). To put this into perspective, consider that recreation related personal income in Illinois increased from $415 million in 1980 to more than $2.3 billion in 2000 (figure 67).

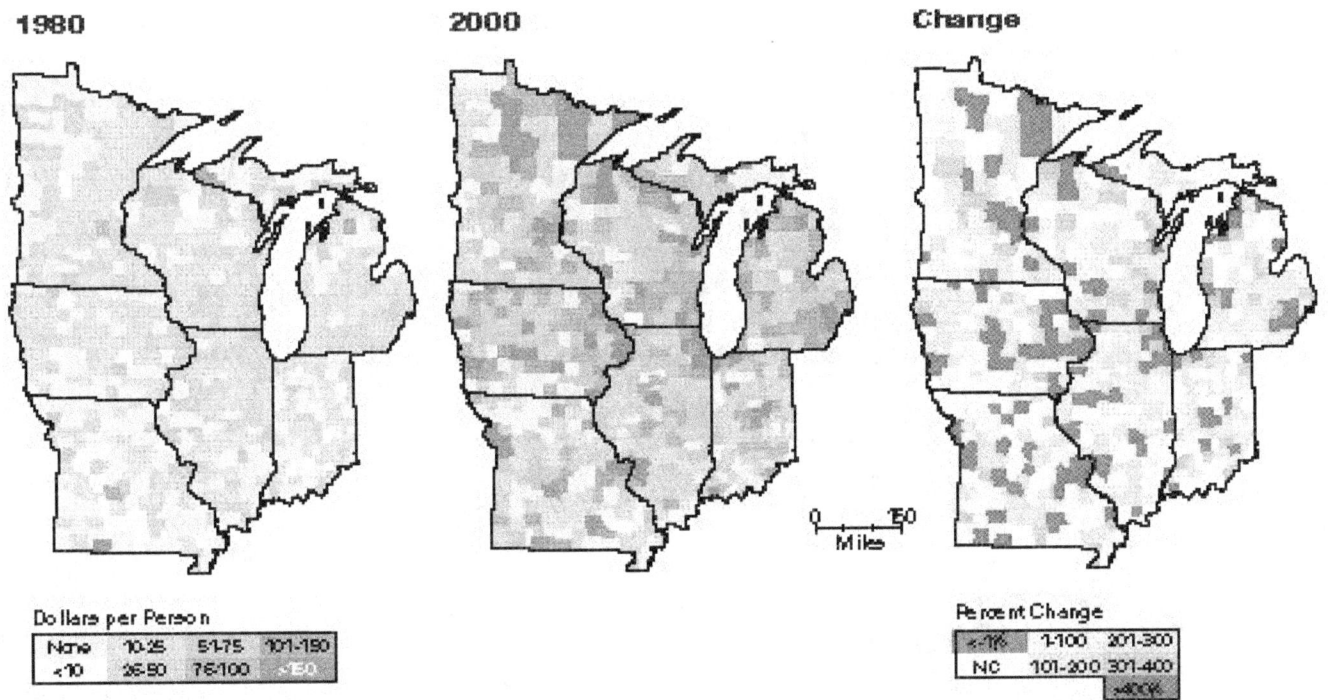

Dollars per Person

None	10-25	51-75	101-150
<10	26-50	76-100	>150

Percent Change

<-1%	1-100	201-300
NC	101-200	301-400
		>400%

Figure 65. Per capita income from amusement and recreation, 1980 and 2000. Percent change in per capita income, 1980-2000. Data source: U.S. Bureau of Economic Analysis.

Percent Change

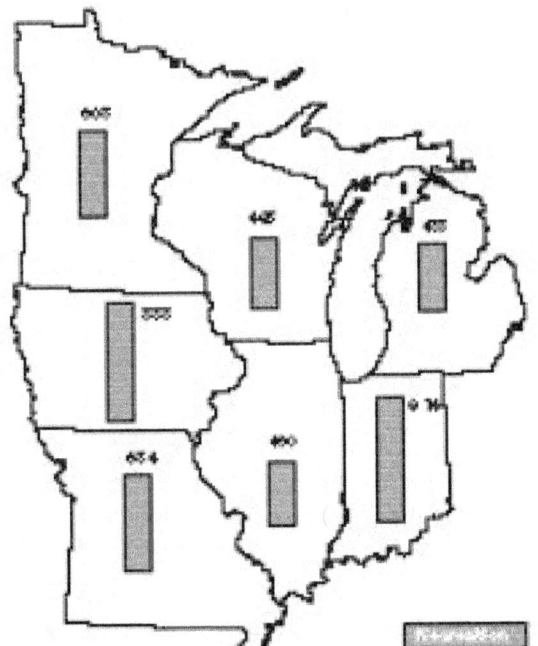

Figure 66. Percent change in personal income from amusement and recreation, 1980-2000. Data source: U.S. Bureau of Economic Analysis.

Change
(million dollars)

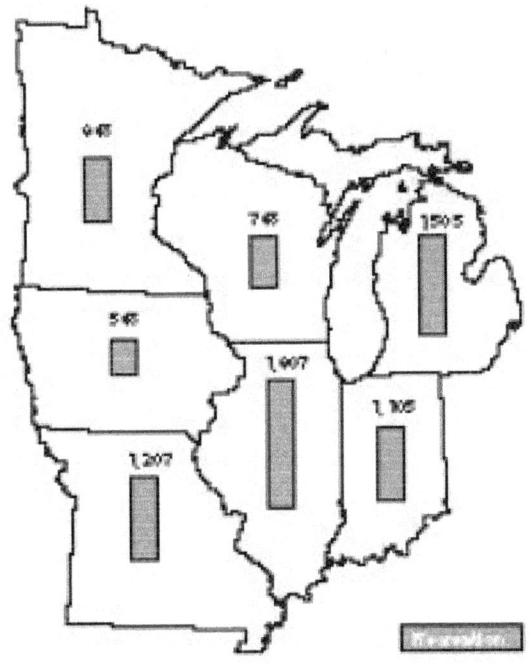

Figure 67. Change in personal income from amusement and recreation (million dollars), 1980-2000. Data source: U.S. Bureau of Economic Analysis.

How Have Attitudes About the Environment Changed?

Attitudes about the environment have changed dramatically since the late 1960s. Clearly, concern about the intensity and extent to which people have developed the biophysical landscape is at an all time high. More to the point, people are concerned about the ecological consequences that landscape change has on the land, water, and air. It should be noted that most everyone shares these concerns. In covering these issues the media tend to paint a dramatic picture of "resource developers" versus "environmentalists." To be sure, conflict exists regarding how to address the negative impacts of landscape change, but it is often greatly exaggerated (Potts 2001).

While there are many types of landscape change, people are generally most familiar with and most concerned about urban sprawl. As noted previously, a recent series of polls indicates that "concern about sprawl" and "crime and violence" are among the most frequently cited local problems in America (Pew Center for Civic Journalism 2000). These results are certainly meaningful; however, they are not very specific, which is problematic because it is difficult for planners, managers, and public officials to respond to general concerns.

Concerns About Sprawl: 1995–2001

To identify specific concerns that people have about sprawl, and to determine whether or not and how those concerns vary across the region and over time, we conducted a computer-guided content analysis of 36,000 news stores about sprawl from 111 news sources, including 11 national media outlets and 94 local newspapers, that were continuously available between 1995 and 2001 (Bengston et al. 2004). Three themes emerged. First, an increased level of concern about sprawl was evident throughout the region (figure 68).

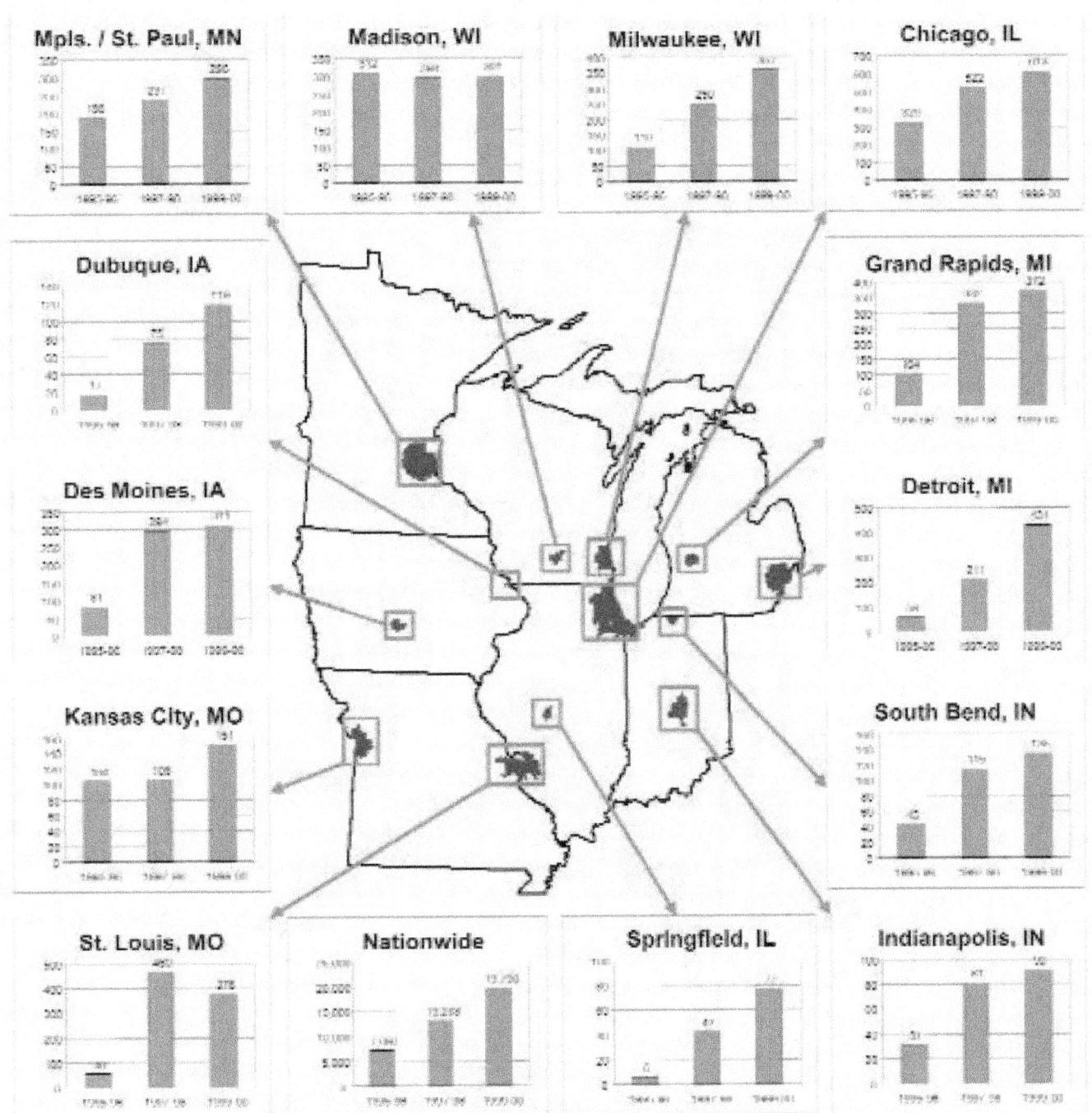

Figure 68. Concern about urban sprawl in 13 metropolitan areas in the Midwest Region and nationwide, 1995-2000. The Y-axis ("Sprawl Concern") is the number of paragraphs in our database of news media stories expressing any of the nine concerns about sprawl.

Environmental and Societal Concerns About Sprawl

Second, we found that concern about sprawl could be classified into two categories: environmental and societal. In all, eight specific concerns about sprawl emerged. In order, the most frequently mentioned concerns about sprawl were related to environmental impacts, loss of farmland, loss of open space, traffic problems, urban decline, sprawl subsidies, loss of a sense of community, and loss of historic sites (figure 69).

Regional and National Concerns About Sprawl

Finally, we found that people across the Midwest generally expressed the same specific concerns about sprawl in roughly the same proportion, and that these concerns were consistent with national trends (figure 69). In particular, concern about the environment or the loss of farmland ranked as the primary concern in each of the 13 major metropolitan areas within the region. There were, however, a few exceptions. For example, expressions of concern that sprawl contributes to urban decay and is subsidized by taxpayers occurred at a much higher rate in Kansas City and St. Louis than in the other metropolitan areas of the region or at the national level.

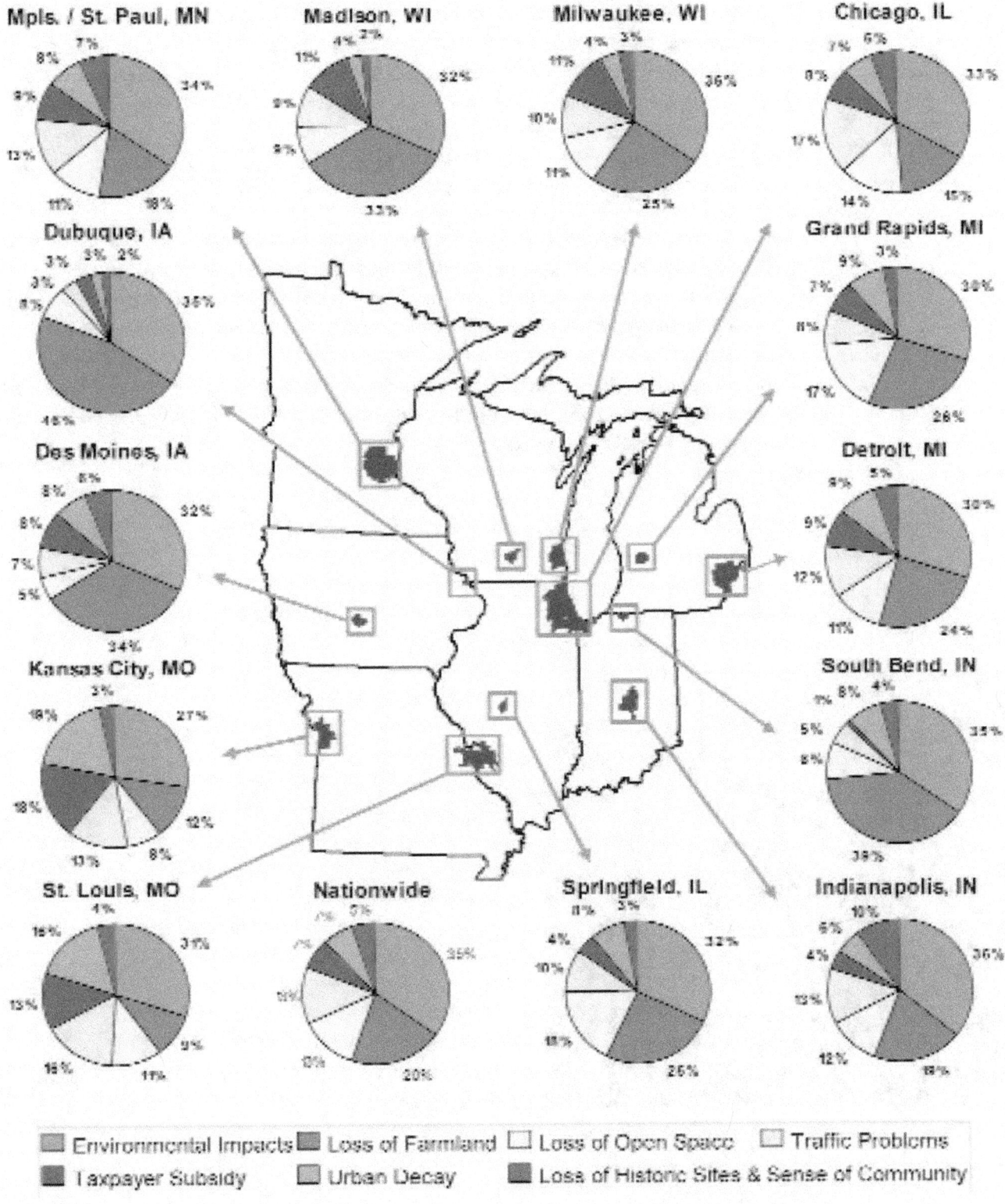

Figure 69. Major concerns about sprawl in 13 metropolitan areas in the Midwest Region and nationwide, 1995-2000.

Legend:
- Environmental Impacts
- Loss of Farmland
- Loss of Open Space
- Traffic Problems
- Taxpayer Subsidy
- Urban Decay
- Loss of Historic Sites & Sense of Community

Summary

The initial goal of the Landscape Change Integrated Research Program is to characterize the intensity, rate, and spatial distribution of changes on the biophysical and social landscapes of the seven Midwestern States. This assessment partially fulfills that goal. Additional data are available on the Changing Midwest Web site at www.ncrs.fs.fed.us/4153/deltawest. Still more data are being processed, including data that describe changes in agricultural land cover, prevalence of oak decline and oak mortality, distribution of insect defoliators and invasive species, relative abundance of additional bird species, road density, and ozone concentration, to name just a few.

As we have noted throughout this document, it is not our intent to characterize change as "good" or "bad." Rather, our aim has been to provide the public, resource professionals, and elected officials with data, images, and just enough context, so they can make their own interpretation. Having said that, we can report that many people have expressed surprise that things are not as bad as they had thought. In particular, people have been encouraged to discover that the area of forest has actually increased, and that the prevalence of large-diameter trees has increased. We hope that you find the assessment useful, and that you will contact any of the authors if you have questions or suggestions about the work they have done.

Ongoing Research

The final section of this paper highlights ongoing landscape change research that is being conducted at the North Central Research Station. The following studies were selected because they are representative of our efforts to: (1) characterize change at finer scales; (2) identify the key "drivers" that influence the rate, extent, and spatial distribution of landscape change; (3) determine the effects of landscape change on people and ecosystems; and (4) project what the biophysical and social landscapes of the region will look like in the future.

Developing Tools to Monitor and Map Forest Fragmentation

The first of these studies describes how we are using existing land cover data sets to monitor the rate, extent, and spatial distribution of forest fragmentation across the region. We are interested in fragmentation because it offers a fine-scale view of how forested land is changing, and because it provides insights that will help us identify key ecological drivers of landscape change.

Fragmentation is the disruption of the continuity of the forest in space that occurs when large blocks of forest are broken up into smaller disjunct fragments or perforated by openings that reduce the area of forest, but do not create a disjunct surface. Fragmentation is relevant because it has significant ecological consequences (Lord and Norton 1990, D'Eon et al. 2002). Whether those consequences are positive or negative is a matter of interpretation, given that there are some plant and animal species that benefit from fragmentation and others that respond negatively. In any event, it is our job to develop information and tools that can be used to decide when and where fragmentation is "good" and when and where it is "bad."

We are currently developing several indices of forest fragmentation so we can map the historical and current extent and spatial distribution of forest fragmentation. For example, we are also utilizing GISfrag (Ripple et al. 1991) to calculate an index of forest fragmentation. In this approach we utilize the 1980 land cover data (LUDA) and USGS National Land Cover Data (NLCD) from 1992 described in Section 1. GISfrag calculates fragmentation as the average distance of forested cells from predominantly non-forested cells, regardless of whether the non-forested cell is an external edge or an internal perforation. For example, consider Ontonagon County, Michigan, which is heavily forested. The land cover data depict a landscape that is completely dominated by forest (figure 70A), whereas our estimate of fragmentation (figure 70B) depicts a forested landscape that is comprised of "core" and "edge" habitat because of non-forest habitats outside the area shown.

Forest fragmentation is relevant because it has significant ecological consequences. Whether those consequences are positive or negative is a matter of interpretation, given that there are some plant and animal species that benefit from fragmentation and others that respond negatively...It is our job to develop information and tools that the public, resource professionals, and public officials can use to decide when and where fragmentation is "good" and when and where it is "bad."

Identifying Drivers of Landscape Change

A second goal of the Landscape Change Integrated Research Program is to identify the factors that influence the rate, extent, and spatial distribution of landscape change. We believe that the key drivers of change in the Midwest are ecological, economic, and social in nature, and we are using linear models to evaluate competing hypotheses

A. 1980 Land Cover

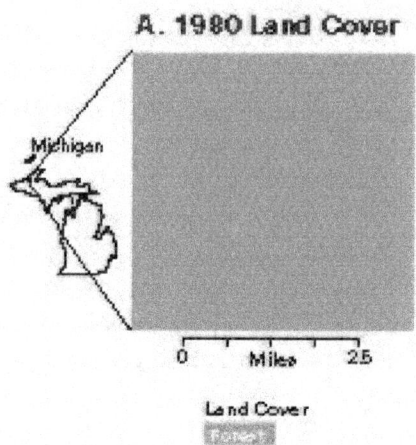

Michigan

0   Miles   2.5

Land Cover
Forest

B. Index of Fragmentation

Distance to Forest Edge
(meters)

| <4,500 | 6,001-7,500 |
| 4,501-6,000 | >7,500 |

Figure 70. Maps depict a 4 square mile tract of land in Ontonagon County, Michigan. Map (A) depicts dominant landcover at a resolution of 1-km². Map (B) depicts an estimate of forest fragmentation.

about the factors that are believed to be driving change using a strength-of-evidence approach.

The first of these studies explores the ecological drivers of landscape change (Gustafson et al., in review). Specifically, we are testing the hypothesis that people decide where they will live, vacation, or retire—thereby changing the landscape—at least partly based on natural amenities, such as the presence and abundance of lakes and forests, and proximity to lands that are reserved from development.

Although developing models may sound like an abstract, academic exercise, the outcome is very practical—these models allow us to identify whether or not ecological characteristics of the landscape are good predictors of where landscape change is likely to occur; assess the relative importance of various ecological factors; and determine if the key ecological drivers of change vary across the region. Importantly, these data will also provide the foundation for developing models that will allow us to predict where future change is likely to occur.

In addition to the ecological drivers study, we are working with research partners from Oregon State University and the USDA Forest Service Pacific Northwest Research Station to explore the economic drivers of landscape change (Haight et al. 2003).

Evaluating Consequences of Change

Another of our goals is to determine the effects or consequences of landscape change on people and ecosystems. For example, we are working to identify if and how landscape change is related to declines in breeding bird populations (see www.ncrs.fs.fed.us/4153/deltawest/landcover/RelativeAbundance.html). We are also investigating linkages between the intensity and spatial distribution of lakeshore development and changes in water quality (see www.ncrs.fs.fed.us/4153/deltawest/landcover/WaterQuality.html).

What Will Landscapes Look Like in the Future?

The final goal of the Landscape Change Integrated Research Program involves predicting what landscapes will look like in the future, and evaluating the effectiveness of alternative strategies for managing change. We are currently developing separate lines of research to predict what the biophysical and social landscapes of the Midwest will look like in the future.

Developing Simulation Models

The first effort involves LANDIS, a program that simulates the effects of interacting forces on the distribution of many forest attributes, including tree

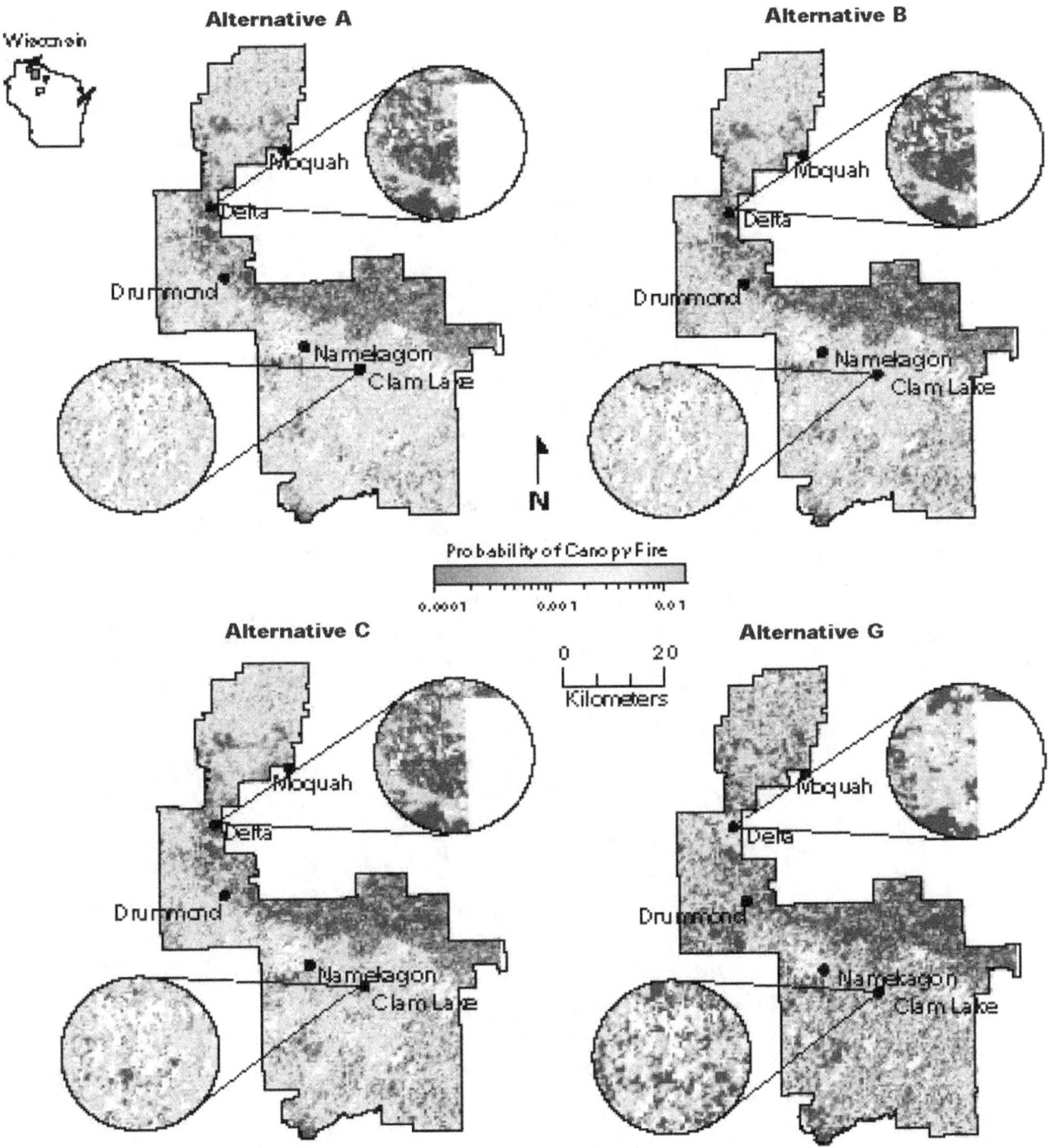

Figure 71. Maps showing the probability (per decade) of canopy fire across the 50 replicate simulations for four alternatives, selected to show the range of canopy fire risk. The alternatives are displayed left to right and top to bottom in descending order of average fire probability. Insets show the 5-km radius area analyzed around two towns in the urban-wildland interface having markedly different response to the no-harvest alternative. Excerpted from Gustafson *et al.* (2004) and used with authors' permission.

species and age classes, tree volume, risk of fire, and suitability as wildlife habitat. Although LANDIS is currently being used with great effectiveness to explore the consequences of alternative forest management practices (Gustafson et al., 2004), and provide insights into what the biophysical landscape of the Midwest will look like in the future (figure 71, page 75), efforts are ongoing to improve the capabilities of these models.

The next generation of LANDIS (v4.0) will improve upon existing modules, and incorporate new modules that can be turned on or off depending on the research question and the availability of input data. In particular, improvements to the fire module will allow simulation of a greater range of fire regimes. Other improvements include a fuel module that models essential linkages between succession, disturbance, and fuel quality and accumulation; a biomass module that tracks biomass pools for each species cohort as well as dead biomass, which will provide more realistic successional dynamics and fuel accumulation on a given site; and a biological disturbance agent module that simulates disturbances via insects and diseases.

Mapping Social Landscapes of the Future

Finally, we have teamed up with scientists from the University of Wisconsin-Madison to pioneer the development of new demographic methods that make it possible to reconstruct past patterns of residential density at the sub-county scale, and make realistic, fine-scale projections decades into the future.

Sub-county Housing Density Change: 1940-2000

To date we have used these innovative methods to trace changes in housing density at the sub-county level across the seven Midwestern States for the past 60 years (figure 72). These backcasted images show that growth has, and is impacting urban, suburban, and rural areas alike. Over this time period, the number of housing units more than doubled, with mid-level housing densities (4-16 units/km^2) increasing the most in terms of the area of land affected. We also determined that low-density development started to become widespread in the forested rural and exurban regions of northern Minnesota, Wisconsin, and Michigan, and southern Missouri during the 1970s, and that by 2000 more than two-thirds of all midwestern forests contained at least 4 housing units/km^2. Finally, we noted contrasting patterns of growth in urban centers and small cities. While major urban centers grew little after the 1940s, their associated suburban areas continued to grow throughout the period. By contrast, most smaller cities, towns, and rural areas of the farm belt grew slowly or not all between 1940 and 2000.

Understanding the Past to Predict the Future

This was not, however, merely an academic exercise in mapping the history of the region. Rather, these maps are accurate enough to use in making resource management decisions and in support of ecological research. In particular, we are using this information to identify hotspots of housing growth; to better understand the nature of the relationship between changes in timber harvest and housing density; to assess changes in the spatial pattern of housing developments over time and in relation to forest resources; to examine potential impacts on wildlife; to identify areas that are at increased risk of fire; and to map the wildland urban interface (figure 73), the area where houses and wildland vegetation meet. Importantly, these data also provide a robust base that we are using to make realistic, fine-scale housing density projections decades into the future.

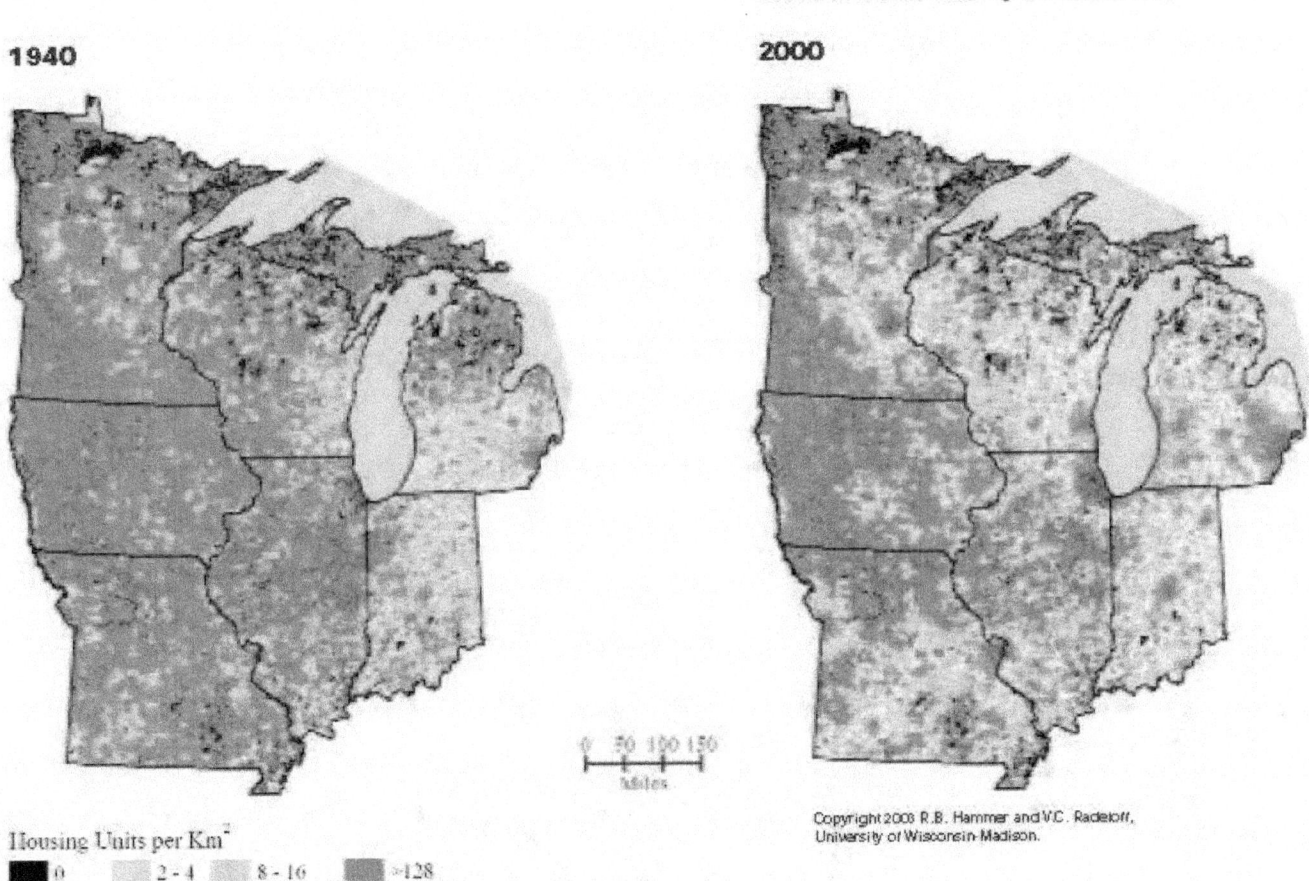

Housing Density Change 1940-2000
Partial Block Group Resolution

1940

2000

0   50 100 150
Miles

Copyright 2003 R.B. Hammer and V.C. Radeloff,
University of Wisconsin-Madison.

Housing Units per Km²

■ 0	2 - 4	8 - 16	>128
0 - 2	4 - 8	16 - 128	Water

Figure 72. Housing density (units/km²), 1940 and 2000. Analysis and image production: R.B. Hammer and V.C. Radeloff, University of Wisconsin-Madison.

How to Contact the Authors

Contact information for the authors of this paper is available on the North Central Research Station Web site at www.ncrs.fs.fed.us; simply select Contact Us from the navigation bar. To learn more about these and other studies, please consider visiting the Web sites of our individual research work units, which can also be accessed from the home page of the North Central Research Station's Web site. Once there, navigate to Our Research Results in Plain Language for an easy-to-read summary of our most recent work.

In closing, we hope that you sense our passion for conserving and restoring the tremendous biophysical and social resources of the Midwest. And we hope that you will join us as advisory clients and working partners in this effort. The USDA Forest Service is committed to Caring for the Land and Serving People, and we at the North Central Research Station are committed to doing Science for People's Sake.

Figure 73. The Wildland-Urban interface in the North Central Region, 2000. Copyright 2003, R.B. Hammer and V.C. Radeloff, University of Wisconsin-Madison.

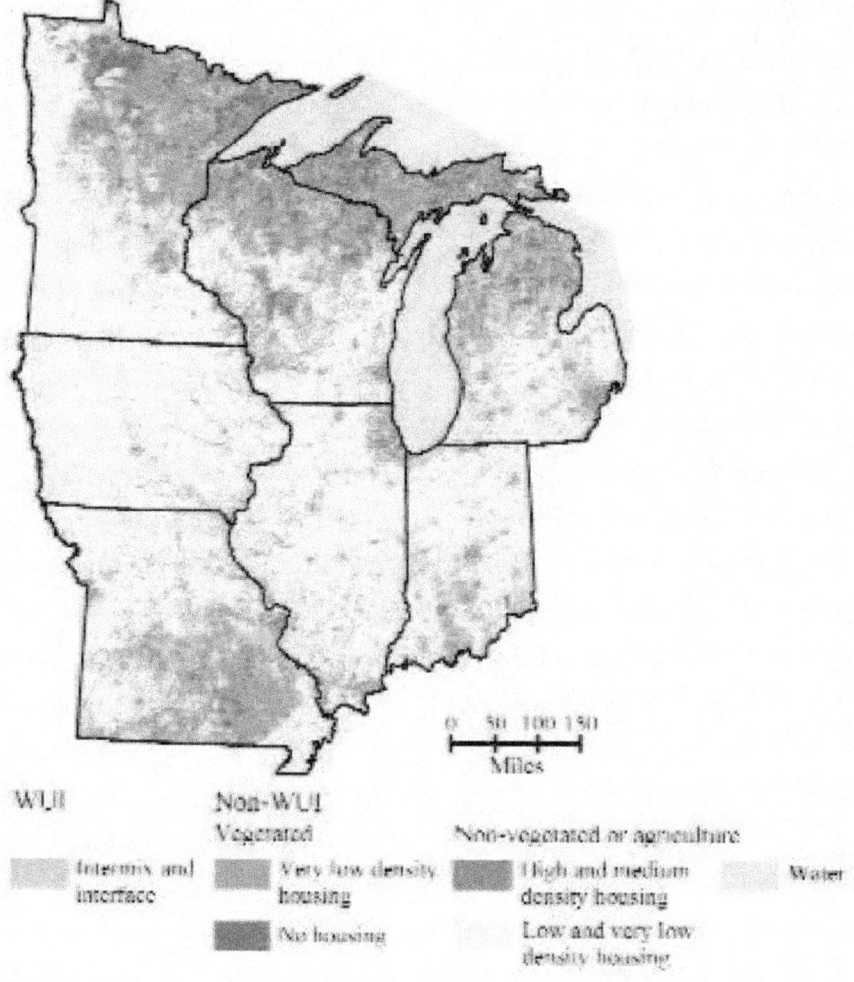

Acknowledgments

This assessment was truly an interdisciplinary and collaborative effort. Many people within the North Central Research Station and at partner institutions contributed to this project. We are grateful to Dennis May, Tom Schmidt, Lisa Earle, Gary Brand, and John Vissage from the Forest Inventory and Analysis unit for their intellectual contributions and for lending their expertise in querying the Forest Inventory and Analysis Database. Sue Lietz, Joy Rasmussen, and Brian Miranda from the Landscape Ecology unit were responsible for data retrieval and archiving, and produced the images that so graphically depict how the landscape of the Midwest has changed. We are also appreciative of the contribution of Willie Suchy, Iowa Department of Natural Resources; John Kube, Illinois Department of Natural Resources; Jim Mitchell, Indiana Division of Fish and Wildlife; John Urbain, Michigan Department of Natural Resources; Mark S. Lenarz, Minnesota Forest Wildlife Populations Research; Lonnie Hansen, Missouri Conservation Department; and Robert E. Rolley, Wisconsin Department of Natural Resources, each of whom provided wildlife data and assisted in its interpretation. John Dwyer, Lucy Burde, and Mary Peterson of the North Central Research Station provided technical and editorial suggestions along the way. Finally, we appreciate the leadership and encouragement provided by Paul Gobster and Bob Haight, co-science leaders of the Landscape Change Integrated Research Program, and by Dave Shriner, to whom we dedicate this atlas.

References

Alverson, W.S.; Waller, D.M.; Solheim, S.L. 1988. Forests to deer: edge effects in northern Wisconsin. Conservation Biology. 2: 348-358.

Bergen, Kathleen M.; Brown, D.G.; Rutherford, J.R.; Gustafson, E. 2002. Development of a method for remote sensing of land-cover change 1980-2000 in the USFS North Central Region using heterogeneous USGS LUDA and NOAA AVHRR 1 km data. In: International geoscience and remote sensing symposium, 24th Canadian symposium on remote sensing: integrating our view of the planet; 2002 June 24-28; Toronto, Canada.

Bengston, D.; Potts, R.S.; Fan, D.; Goetz, E. 2004. Monitoring concern about urban sprawl: a computer content analysis of the public debate. In: Wildland-Urban interface: forum on economics and policy; 2004 March 14; St. Augustine, FL.

Caudill, J.; Laughland, A. 1998. U.S. Fish & Wildlife Service 1996 National and State Economic Impacts of Wildlife Watching: based on the 1996 National Survey of Fishing, Hunting and Wildlife-Associated Recreation.

Craven, S. 2002. University of Wisconsin-Madison. Chronic wasting disease timeline. [online] URL: www.news.wisc.edu/cwd/timeline.html

D'Eon, R.G.; Glenn, S.M.; Parfitt, I.; Fortin, M.-J. 2002. Landscape connectivity as a function of scale and organism vagility in a real forested landscape. Conservation Ecology. 6(2): 10 [online] URL: http://www.consecol.org/vol6/iss2/art10

Gross, J.E.; Miller, M.W. 2001. CWD in mule deer: a model of disease dynamics, control options, and population consequences. Journal of Wildlife Management. 65: 205-215.

Gustafson, E.J. 1998. Clustering timber harvests and the effect of dynamic forest management policy on forest fragmentation. Ecosystems. 1: 484-492.

Gustafson, E.J.; Zollner, P.A.; He, H.S.; Sturtevant, B.R.; Mladenoff, D.J. 2004. Influence of forest management alternatives and landtype on susceptibility to fire in northern Wisconsin, USA. Landscape Ecology. 19: 327-341.

Gustafson, E.J.; Hammer, R.B.; Radeloff, V.C.; Potts, R.S. In Review. The relationship between environmental amenities and human settlement patterns between 1980 and 2000 in the Midwestern USA.

Johnson, K.M.; Beale, C.L. 2002. Nonmetro recreation counties: their identification and rapid growth. Rural America. 17(4): 12-19.

Laplanche, J.L.; Hunter, N.; Shinagawa, M.; Williams, E. 1999. Scrapie, chronic wasting disease, and transmissible mink encephalopathy. Prusiner, Stanley B. Prion-biology-and-diseases. Cold Spring Harbor, NY: Cold Spring Harbor Laboratory Press.

Lord, J.M.; Norton, D.A. 1990. Scale and the spatial concept of fragmentation. Conservation Biology. 4(2): 197-202.

Miles, P.D.; Brand, G.J.; Alerich, C.L.; Bednar, L.F.; Woudenberg, S.W.; Glover, J.F.; Ezzell, E.N. 2001. The Forest Inventory and Analysis database: database description and users manual version 1.0. Gen. Tech. Rep. NC-218. St. Paul, MN: U.S. Department of Agriculture, Forest Service, North Central Research Station.130 p.

Miller, M.W.; Wild, M.A.; Williams, E.S. 1998. Epidemiology of chronic wasting disease in captive Rocky Mountain elk. Journal of Wildlife Diseases. 34: 532-538.

Pelij, J. 2002. Understanding chronic wasting disease in Wisconsin: the first step to disease control. PUB-WM-399 2002 JG.

Pew Center for Civic Journalism. 2000. Straight talk from Americans, 2000: national survey results. Washington, DC: Pew Foundation. [online] URL: www.pewcenter.org/doingcj/research/r_ST2000.html

Potts, R.S. 2001. The nature of social assessment in an era of collaborative management. Missoula, MT: University of Montana. Ph.D. dissertation.

Ripple, W.J.; Bradshaw, G.A.; Spies, T.A. 1991. Measuring landscape pattern in the Cascade Range of Oregon, USA. Biological Conservation. 57: 73-88.

Riitters, K.; Wickham, J.; O'Neill, R.; Jones, B.; Smith, E. 2000. Global-scale patterns of forest fragmentation. Conservation Ecology. 4(2): 3. [online] URL: http://www.consecol.org/vol4/iss2/art3

Riitters, K.H.; Wickham, J.D.; O'Neill, R.V.; Jones, K.B.; Smith, E.R.; Coulston, J.W.; Wade, T.G.; Smith, J.H. 2002. Fragmentation of continental United States Forests. Ecosystems. 5: 815-822.

Sauer, J.R.; Hines, J.E.; Fallon, J. 2003. The North American Breeding Bird Survey, results and analysis 1966 - 2002. Version 2003.1. Laurel, MD: USGS Patuxent Wildlife Research Center.

Shifley, S.R.; Sullivan, N.H. 2002. The status of timber resources in the North Central United States. Gen. Tech. Rep. NC-228. St. Paul, MN: U.S. Department of Agriculture, Forest Service, North Central Research Station. 47 p.

Thompson, F.R.; Sauer, J.R.; Pagen, R.W.; Potts, R.S. 2003. Is landscape change driving declines in breeding bird populations in the North Central United States? In: Society for Conservation Biology. 17th annual meeting; 2003 June 28-July 2; Duluth, MN.

U.S. Department of Agriculture, Forest Service. 2001. 2000 RPA assessment of forest and range lands. FS-687. Washington, DC: U.S. Department of Agriculture, Forest Service. 76 p. http://www.fs.fed.us/pl/rpa/rpaassess.pdf

Williams, E.S.; Young, S. 1980. Chronic wasting disease of captive mule deer: a spongiform encephalopathy. Journal of Wildlife Diseases. 16: 89-98.

Williams, E.S.; Young, S. 1992. Spongiform encephalopathies of Cervidae. Scientific and Technical Review Office of International Epizootics. 11: 551-567.

Web Sites

Advanced Very High Resolution Radiometer (AVHRR), NOAA National Data Centers, NGDC, www.ngdc.noaa.gov/seg/globsys/avhrr.shtml

Applied Population Laboratory, University of Wisconsin-Madison, www.ssc.wisc.edu/poplab/

Bureau of Economic Analysis, U.S. Department of Commerce, www.bea.doc.gov

Bureau of Labor Statistics, U.S. Department of Labor, www.bls.gov

Chronic Wasting Disease: The Disease and its management in Wisconsin, www.news.wisc.edu/cwd/timeline.html

Forest Inventory and Analysis Research Unit, USDA Forest Service North Central Research Station, http://www.ncrs.fs.fed.us/4801/

Forest Inventory and Analysis Database (FIADB), USDA Forest Service North Central Research Station, http://www.ncrs.fs.fed.us/4801/fiadb/index.htm

Harvest for Windows: Timber Harvest Simulation Model, Version 6.0, http://www.ncrs.fs.fed.us/4153/Harvest/v60/Harv60_User.pdf

Landscape Ecology Research Work Unit (RWU 4153), USDA Forest Service North Central Research Station, http://www.ncrs.fs.fed.us/4153/

Lexis-Nexis online database, www.lexis-nexis.com/

National Aerial Photography Program (NAPP), USGS, www.edc.usgs.gov/products/aerial/napp.html

National Land Cover Data (NLCD), USGS, http://landcover/usgs.gov/mapping_proc.html

Natural Environments for Urban Populations Research Work Unit (RWU 4902), USDA Forest Service, North Central Research Station, www.ncrs.fs.fed.us/4902/

North American Breeding Bird Survey, USGS, www.mbr-pwrc.usgs.gov/bbs/intro00.html

Patuxent Wildlife Research Center, USGS, www.pwrc.usgs.gov/

Pew Center for Civic Journalism, www.pewcenter.org

School of Natural Resources and the Environment, University of Michigan, www.snre.umich.edu/

The Changing Midwest Assessment: Land Cover, Natural Resources and People, www.ncrs.fs.fed.us/4153/deltawest/

Threatened, Endangered and Sensitive Species Program, USDA Forest Service, www.fs.fed.us/r9/wildlife/tes/incex.html

U.S. Census Bureau, U.S. Department of Commerce, www.census.gov

Glossary of Terms

Amusement and recreation–A class of service sector jobs that the Bureau of Economic Analysis and Bureau of Labor Statistics use to track changes in the U.S. economy.

Chronic wasting disease–Chronic wasting disease of the deer family is a transmissible spongiform encephalopathy (TSE), a member of infectious diseases, including scrapie (found in sheep) and "mad cow" disease, which affect animals and people. CWD is characterized by weight loss and behavioral changes; it invariably results in death.

Conservation economy–Refers to an economy that strives to balance social capital, natural capital, and economic capital.

Forest land–Land that is at least 10 percent stocked by forest trees of any size, or formerly having had such tree cover, and not currently developed for nonforest use. Note: Stocking is measured by comparing specified standards with basal area and/or number of trees, age or size, and spacing. The minimum area for classification of forest land is 1 acre. Roadside, streamside, and shelterbelt strips of timber must have a crown width of at least 120 feet for a continuous 365 feet to qualify as forest land. Unimproved roads and trails, streams, or other bodies of water or clearings in forest areas shall be classed as forest if less than 120 feet wide.

Forestland cover type–Indicates trees are the dominant feature on the landscape. As a rule of thumb, a tract of land will not be classed as forestland unless it has a canopy closure of at least 40 percent.

Forest type–A classification of forest land in which the named species, either singly or in combination, makes up a plurality of live tree stocking. These types are based on a standard set of local forest types in the Forest Service Handbook and have been logically organized into broader forest type groups to facilitate reporting.

Frontier economy–Refers to an economy that is based on resource extraction and development.

Lumber and wood products/forestry–Classes of manufacturing sector jobs that the Bureau of Economic Analysis and Bureau of Labor Statistics use to track changes in the U.S. economy.

Permanent housing–The U.S. Census Bureau defines a housing unit as a house, apartment, group of rooms, or single room that is occupied or intended for occupancy as separate living quarters.

Private industrial timberland–An ownership class of private lands where the land owner operates a primary wood processing plant, which is defined to include commercial operations that originate the primary processing of wood on a regular and continuous basis, such as pulp or paper mills, sawmills, panel board mills, or post and pole mills.

Private non-industrial timberland–An ownership class of private lands where the owner does not operate wood-using plants.

Seasonal housing–The U.S. Census Bureau defines seasonal housing units as living quarters that are held for weekend or other occasional use throughout the year; second homes may or may not be classified as seasonal housing units.

Stand-size class–A classification of the predominant (based on stocking) diameter class of live trees on forest land. Large-diameter trees are at least 11.0 inches diameter for hardwoods and at least 9.0 inches diameter for softwoods. Medium-diameter trees are at least 5.0 inches diameter but not as large as large-diameter trees. Small-diameter trees are less than 5.0 inches diameter.

Stocking–Tree stocking. A relative term used to describe (in percent) the density of trees on a given stand, and the adequacy of a given stand density in meeting specific management objectives. Stands may be Overstocked (100+%), Fully stocked (60-99%), Medium stocked (35-59%), Poorly stocked (10-34%), or Nonstocked (0-9%).

Timberland–Forest land that is producing, or is capable of producing, in excess of 20 cubic feet per acre per year of industrial roundwood products under natural conditions, is not withdrawn from timber utilization by statute or administrative regulation, and is not associated with urban or rural development.

Urban land cover–A mixture of buildings, conveyances, and associated vegetation that is indicative of human settlement, and industrial or commercial activity.

Appendix A: FIA Periodic Inventories

The data we used to monitor county- and State-level change in forest characteristics originated from periodic inventories between 1974 and 1998. The Forest Inventory and Analysis unit currently conducts annual inventories. For additional information refer to Miles *et al.* 2001; [online] URL: http://www.ncrs.fs.fed.us/4801/

State	Cycle 2	Cycle 3	Cycle 4	Cycle 5
Illinois		1985	1998	
Indiana		1986	1998	
Iowa	1974	1990		
Michigan			1980	1993
Minnesota			1977	1990
Missouri		1972	1989	
Wisconsin			1983	1996

Appendix B: Structure of Midwestern Forests

Area of large-, medium-, and small-diameter timberland (acres) by forest type group, 1980 and 2000.
Data source: FIADB; [online] URL: http://www.ncrs.fs.fed.us/4801/fiadb/index.html

	1980 (acres)			2000 (acres)		
	Large	Medium	Small	Large	Medium	Small
Oak/Hickory	9,866,689	6,992,779	3,762,094	11,956,200	5,817,400	3,183,900
Maple/Beech/Birch	6,327,218	5,264,566	2,743,545	8,834,800	5,858,700	3,170,200
Aspen/Birch	2,242,900	7,563,400	4,446,000	3,199,600	4,789,000	4,907,900
Spruce/Fir	1,341,400	3,218,100	2,328,200	1,768,400	2,729,500	3,072,500
Elm/Ash/Cottonwood	2,737,083	2,206,004	1,273,975	3,382,100	2,219,100	1,523,000
All Forest Types	24,436,889	27,420,182	15,767,881	31,810,700	23,444,200	17,222,200

Appendix C: Identification and Life History of Midwestern Birds

Northern Cardinal

The northern cardinal is unmistakable among midwestern birds, especially the male, with its bright red plumage, distinctive crest, and red bill. The northern cardinal is a permanent resident that breeds in successional-scrub habitat. It is a ground or low nesting bird with a diet consisting mostly of seeds and fruit. Identification and life history data compiled by Gregory Gough, Patuxent Wildlife Research Center, www.mbr-pwrc.usgs.gov/id/framlst/i5930id.html

Henslow's Sparrow

The Henslow's sparrow is a small bird with a flat head, large conical bill, and a short tail. It has two dark "whiskers", a buffy streaked breast and sides, a white belly and under tail coverts, and a narrow, whitish crown stripe. It can be distinguished from other sparrows by its olive face and rusty wings. The Henslow's sparrow is a short distance migrant that breeds in grassland habitat. It is a ground or low nesting bird and is often found in open fields with tall herbaceous vegetation. Its diet consists mostly of insects and seeds. Identification and life history data compiled by Gregory Gough, Patuxent Wildlife Research Center, www.mbr-pwrc.usgs.gov/id/framlst/i5470id.html

Wood Thrush

The wood thrush has a rusty crown, nape, and upper back. It has a white-eye ring, streaked cheeks, white under parts with black spots throughout, brown upper parts, and pink legs. It can be distinguished from other thrushes in that it has larger spots that extend onto the belly and contrast between the rusty head and duller brown back. The wood thrush is a neotropical migrant that breeds in woodland habitat. It is a mid-story nester, and has a diet consisting mostly of insects. Identification and life history data compiled by Gregory Gough, Patuxent Wildlife Research Center, www.mbr-pwrc.usgs.gov/id/framlst/i7550id.html

Northern cardinal
Photo courtesy of John Sliwoski –
Backyard Birding

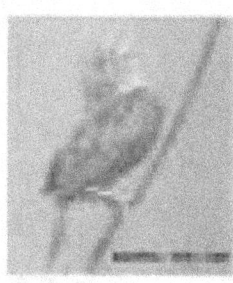

Henslow's sparrow

Wood thrush

Dedication

This atlas is dedicated to Dave Shriner, whose leadership, expertise, support, and good cheer as Assistant Director for Research at the North Central Research Station were critical to the success of North Central's Integrated Research programs and to this project.

About the Authors:

Robert Potts is a Research Ecologist with the North Central Research Station, Rhinelander, Wisconsin.

Eric Gustafson is a Research Ecologist with the North Central Research Station, Rhinelander, Wisconsin.

Susan I. Stewart is a Research Social Scientist with the North Central Research Station, Evanston, Illinois.

Frank R. Thompson is a Research Wildlife Biologist with the North Central Research Station, Columbia, Missouri.

Kathleen Bergen is an Assistant Research Scientist and Adjunct Assistant Professor of Natural Resources with the University of Michigan, Ann Arbor, Michigan.

Daniel G. Brown is an Associate Professor of Natural Resources and Environment with the University of Michigan, Ann Arbor, Michigan.

Roger Hammer is an Assistant Professor of Rural Sociology with the University of Wisconsin, Madison, Wisconsin.

Volker Radeloff is an Assistant Professor of Landscape Ecology with the University of Wisconsin, Madison, Wisconsin.

David Bengston is a Research Social Scientist with the North Central Research Station, St. Paul, Minnesota.

John Sauer is a Research Wildlife Biologist with the USGS Patuxent Wildlife Research Center, Laurel, Maryland.

Brian Sturtevant is a Research Ecologist with the North Central Research Station, Rhinelander, Wisconsin.

Potts, Robert; Gustafson, Eric; Stewart, Susan I.; Thompson, Frank R.; Bergen, Kathleen; Brown, Daniel G.; Hammer, Roger; Radeloff, Volker; Bengston, David; Sauer, John; Sturtevant, Brian.

2004. The Changing Midwest Assessment: land cover, natural resources, and people. Gen. Tech. Rep. NC-250. St. Paul, MN: U.S. Department of Agriculture, Forest Service, North Central Research Station. 87 p.

Documents changes in land cover, forests, selected natural resources, and human demographics and attitudes across the Midwest from roughly 1980 to 2000.

————————————

Key Words: Midwest, landscape change, forests, human demographics, plants, animals.